CELEBRATING OUR EQUALITY

CELEBRATING OUR EQUALITY

A COOKBOOK WITH RECIPES AND REMEMBRANCES FROM HOWARD UNIVERSITY

CAROLYN QUICK TILLERY

CITADEL PRESS
Kensington Publishing Corp.
www.kensingtonbooks.com.

CITADEL PRESS books are published by

Kensington Publishing Corp.
850 Third Avenue
New York, NY 10022

All Kensington titles, imprints, and distributed lines are available at special quantity discounts for bulk purchases for sales promotions, premiums, fund-raising, educational, or institutional use. Special book excerpts or customized printings can also be created to fit specific needs. For details, write or phone the office of the Kensington special sales manager: Kensington Publishing Corp., 850 Third Avenue, New York, NY 10022, attn: Special Sales Department; phone: 1-800-221-2647.

CITADEL PRESS and the Citadel logo are Reg. U.S. Pat. and TM Off.

First printing: November 2003

10 9 8 7 6 5 4 3 2 1

Printed in the United States of America

Library of Congress Control Number 2003106183

ISBN 0-8065-2508-8

As always, I give all glory to God and Jesus Christ my Lord and Savior who goes before me as my Jehovah Nissi or "Banner of Victory" and comes behind as my strong rear guard.

CONTENTS

PREFACE

Equal Rights and Education for All.

—Motto, first seal of Howard University

Celebrating Our Equality is the third in a series of historic cookbooks focusing upon the proud heritage of Historic Black Colleges and Universities (HBCUs). As such, it is a companion piece to *A Taste of Freedom,* a cookbook with recipes and remembrances from the Hampton Institute, and *The African-American Heritage Cookbook,* traditional recipes and fond remembrances from Alabama's renowned Tuskegee Institute.

HBCUs such as Tuskegee, Hampton, Howard, and a host of others owe their existence, in large part, to the vision and courage of Civil War hero Oliver Otis Howard, a founding committee member and the third president of Howard University. General Howard fought on the side of the Union Army to liberate an enslaved people. With the war's end, four million largely destitute and illiterate African-Americans were freed. As one result, Union Generals Grant and Sherman began lobbying for establishment of an institution to address the immediate needs and guarantee the civil rights of freedmen.

In March of 1865, Congress overrode a veto by President Andrew Johnson to establish the Bureau of Refugees, Freedmen and Abandoned Lands. General O.O. Howard was named the bureau's commissioner in 1866. The bureau immediately began fighting for the freedmen's voting rights, enforcing their legal rights, and providing what many viewed as an equal education. As commissioner, General Howard was instrumental in establishing an organized system of universities and colleges to provide basic academic and industrial skills and to train teachers, doctors, and lawyers to serve the rapidly growing African-American communities. Howard soon established the first medical teaching college for African-Americans, and a nondenominational theology department and law school quickly followed. As a direct result of General Howard's commitment to equal rights and education many HBCU graduates would be at the forefront of the civil rights struggle.

Many civil rights victories were won by a young Howard University Law School graduate, Thurgood Marshall. First as a civil rights attorney and then as a U.S. Supreme Court Justice, Marshall dedicated his life to the achievement of equal rights.

Other notable Howard University alumni who continued in this tradition include Andrew Young, civil rights activist, first black U.S representative from Georgia since Reconstruction, ambassador to the U.N., and two-term mayor of Atlanta, Georgia; Stokely Carmichael, civil rights activist; and L. Douglas Wilder, the first African-American since Reconstruction to be elected to the Virginia Legislature and the first black elected to govern a state in U.S. history.

At Howard a prominent and activist faculty inspired students to challenge racism and discrimination. Among them was Dr. Ralph Johnson Bunche, a noted scholar and activist who received the Nobel Peace Prize for his work in the Arab-Israeli War. Following Bunche's participation in the 1963 March on Washington, President John F. Kennedy designated him to receive the Medal of Freedom, our nation's highest civilian award. The NAACP recognized his twenty-two years of organizational service by presenting Dr. Bunche with its highest reward, the Spingarm Medal. Other notable graduates and faculty include Nobel laureate and Pulitzer Prize-winning author, Toni Morrison; writer Zora Neale Hurston; critically acclaimed jazz musician Donald Byrd; singer/composers Roberta Flack and Donny Hathaway; entertainer and business entrepreneur Sean Combs; choreographer, dancer, actress, and producer Debbie Allen, and her sister, actress Phylicia Rashad; opera singer Jessye Norman; Dr. Carter G. Woodson, the father of Black History Month; and a host of others.

Like its companion volumes, this book contains history, vignettes, vintage photographs, and recipes illustrating Howard's heritage and history. The photographs capture moments in history while the narratives tell us of a formerly bound people's struggle for equality. As a result of their struggle, we as a nation continue to consider the true meaning of "equal treatment for all" and continue to make room at the table for those not originally considered by The Founders.

The recipes, photographs, and stories reflect the pioneering spirit of Howard University and the courage of its graduates to fight for social justice. As a result of their struggles we as a nation can celebrate our evolving equality.

ACKNOWLEDGMENTS

Special thanks to my husband, J.R., and daughter Ashley, your love and words of encouragement are the wind beneath my wings.

The author gratefully acknowledges the kind cooperation of Howard University Archivist Dr. Clifford L. Muse, Jr., Assistant Archivist Mr. Theodros "Teddy" Abebe; as well as Ms. Nairobi Abrams, Director of Human Relations and her assistant Ms. Rosemary Darego.

Special thanks to the extended Quick family of Washington, D.C. Your kind hospitality during my research visit was a special blessing to me. So, thanks Aunt Regina, Margaret, John, Judy, David, Dr. Polly Brown and her husband Nathan, who are both proud Howard University graduates who represent their university extremely well in the field of education and their community at large.

Special thanks to Mariel Nanasi, a civil- and human-rights warrior and friend.

Last, but definitely not least, thanks to my Kensington/Citadel family. Bruce, thank you for believing in this series of books, thank you Mickie Searcy and Jessica McClean for promoting them. And thanks, Margaret, for your exceptional editing and friendship. I know there are dozens of others who quietly work behind the scenes, getting the tough jobs done. The pride in your craft is clearly evident and much appreciated.

Prologue: A Heritage Of Leadership

Howard University Produces Leaders for America and a Global Community

Today, we celebrate the 130th Commencement of this great university, steeped in the very finest of Howard's traditions. Pause for just a moment. Take a good look at those sitting near you. This, my colleagues, is what "Leadership for America and the global community" looks like!

This morning, each of you will rise to take the mantle of leadership in your new careers, your continuing academic journeys, your communities, and most important, in your personal crusades to effect significant, positive change.

This very affirmation will be spoken to graduates across the United States in the weeks to come. However, as sons and daughters of Howard University—"the Capstone," "the Mecca,"—this is more than a simple affirmation. It is the deep conviction that will drive you, steer you and—even in the darkest of hours—lift you.

Let me remind you of your legacy. It is not a legacy of names, but a legacy of action—and activism.

It's more than Trustee Frederick Douglass. It is his bold voice that even today speaks out against America's still-peculiar institutions.

It's more than Nobel Laureate Toni Morrison. It is her power to frame creative thought into strong words to tell "our story."

1

It's more than Mordecai Wyatt Johnson. It is the way he taught us to build a community, a nation of unparalleled intellectual capacity, and navigate its unhalted growth through even the most hostile, perilous times.

It's more than Debbie Allen, Phylicia Rashad, and Jessye Norman. It is their ability to dance not only with feet, but with spirit; to sing our song in the strangest of lands; and to portray our images, not as others see us, but as we truly—beautifully—are.

It's more than Patricia Roberts Harris. It is the grace with which she taught us to take a stand and stand strong, to blaze trails through uncharted territory and to lead others through it.

It is more than Vernon Jordan and Spottswood Robinson. It's their Davidian ability to fight injustice, not with rocks of stone, but boulders of righteousness.

Sons and daughters of Howard, yours is a heritage of leadership. Even more, as the product of a *national* university, you are entitled to enter the arena of leadership. What you do with your lives will determine your ability to remain there. I have no doubts that you will. . . .

—Patrick Swygert, President, Howard University,
excerpt from speech given during 1998 Commencement Exercises

Howard: The University

*For wherever and whenever measures are advanced for the welfare of the people
and the direction of the masses there the sons [and daughters] of Howard
will be found in the midst of them.*

—Professor Kelly Miller,
President's Address, Sixth Triennial Meeting of the College Alumni Association
of Howard University, College Chapel, May 18, 1892

A TRADITION OF EXCELLENCE

No more prophetic or truer words could be spoken of Howard University, a predominantly black university founded in 1867, shortly after the end of the Civil War. Named for its third president, Civil War hero General Oliver Otis Howard, Howard University would soon be hailed as the capstone of Negro education. Its sons and daughters would advance to leadership positions in many areas, including social reform, medicine, law, entertainment, education, and government.

HOWARD HISTORY MAKER: Professor Kelly Miller, believed to be the first African-American to study graduate mathematics, was appointed dean of the College of Arts and Sciences in 1907 and on the faculty when, in 1929, faculty members Elbert Frank Cox and Dudley W. Woodward became the first African-Americans to earn a Ph.D. in Mathematics.

Howard University's faculty and alumni roster reads like "who's who" in African-American history: Dr. Charles Drew, Dr. Ralph Johnson Bunche, Justice Thurgood Marshall, Ambassador Andrew Young, Ambassador Patricia Roberts Harris, Governor L. Douglas Wilder, former Washington, D.C., mayor Sharon Pratt Kelly, Vernon Jordan, Howard University President J. Patrick Swygert, Stokely Carmichael, Nobel Laureate and Pulitzer Prize–winner Toni Morrison, Zora Neale Hurston, Debbie Allen, and her sister, actress Phylicia Rashad, to name a very few.

This limited roll call of excellence exemplifies the sentiment expressed by Professor Kelly Miller more than 110 years ago and is emblematic of Howard's history and heritage.

Identifying the Need and Laying the Foundation

The story of Howard University begins shortly after the close of the Civil War. Following emancipation, a great tide of newly freed slaves flooded the District of Columbia. Many of the new arrivals were desperate for food and shelter; most were illiterate and even more were despondent as they faced an uncertain future for which they were ill-prepared.

In mid-November of 1866, ten members of the First Congregational Society of Washington, D.C., were meeting in the home of Dr. Charles Boynton when the discussion turned to the "special obligation of the nation and the clergy to the recently emancipated freedmen." Dr. Boynton proposed establishing a theological seminary for freedmen in Washington, D.C., to train black clergy to provide assistance and spiritual guidance to the freedmen.

On November 20, the group gathered in the home of Deacon Henry Brewster and confirmed the need for a theological school and resolved to establish a seminary to prepare freedmen to minister to nearly four million newly freed slaves and 250,000 free-born blacks. A charter drafted on January 23, 1867, provided for a college only.

(Photograph courtesy Howard University Archives)

Shortly thereafter, the founders also recognized an urgent need for trained physicians who would treat freedmen. Two weeks later, a second draft proposed a university, which would include the following departments: Normal and Preparatory, Collegiate, Theological, Law, Medical, Agriculture, and any other departments desired. Finally, on March 2, 1867, the second draft of the charter was approved by the last session of the Thirty-ninth Congress.

On May 1, 1867, the Normal Department was established to prepare "colored" teachers for schools that were springing up around the country. It opened with four white students, the daughters of two members of the Board of Trustees, and was located in a large frame building on Georgia Avenue just below W, or Pomeroy, Street. A much needed Preparatory School was soon added, as were the Normal and Preparatory Departments, and a Model School, which included elementary grades A, B, C, and D. Finally, an upgraded class was established to prepare students to enter the model school.

In this manner, Howard provided a comprehensive system to meet the educational needs of newly freed slaves. From the very outset, it provided a coeducational and integrated academic environment. By the end of the first term, enrollment increased to 94. Within seven years the curriculum expanded to include the following 11 departments: Normal, Preparatory, Industrial, Theological, Medical, Law, Military, Musical, Agricultural, Commercial, and Night School. In response to increased demand, a committee was formed to secure a new site for the University. According to General Howard:

> *General Whittlesey and myself were sent out by the Board of Trustees as agents to find . . . a site for Howard University, a task at that time not easy to be performed. We went to several places where we thought we might have a reasonable success. At last we came to Mr. Smith. We tried to get the lower part of his ground where the first building, the dance house, stood, but he shook his head and said it would not do. We then tried for the upper portions near the Soldiers' Home. Then after a little mediation, I said, "What, Mr. Smith, will you take for the whole of your estate? How much is there of it?" He answered that there were 150 acres and that he would take $1,000.00 an acre. . . . Though we had not one dollar in the treasury, I said to Mr. Smith, "We will take it, the whole of your farm here, at your price . . ."*

> —General O. O. Howard

Finding themselves too land rich and cash poor to develop a suitable campus, the trustees raised money by selling some of the excess property.

As General Howard recalled, "All of the land was soon platted and put on sale at a price averaging some four times the cost of the purchase. . . . The most was sold; [however, the] park

GARDNER, Photographer.   511 7th Street, Washington.

HOWARD UNIVERSITY.
(SOUTH-EAST FRONT.)

(Photograph courtesy Howard University Archives)

was reserved and the grounds, as they now exist, for the buildings. . . . The sandpit was used for manufacturing the brick out of which several of the buildings, Balloch's house and mine, were constructed. . . ." Within three years, the school sold $172,000.00 worth of property. Dr. Howard reported, "[At] any rate, what came from the land, from funds and from donations straight from the people enabled our treasurer to meet the first payment when it became due." By 1873, campus buildings included the Medical School building (completed in 1869) and hospital, the main or "University" building, and Miner Hall, all of which were constructed by the Freedmen's Bureau and later presented to the university as a gift. The remainder of the campus consisted of Clark and Spaulding Halls and several faculty houses.

Howard: The Man

Less than a month after the weary Emancipator passed to his rest, his successor assigned Major-Gen. Oliver O. Howard to duty as Commissioner of the new Bureau. He was a Maine man, then only thirty-five years of age. He had marched with Sherman to the sea, had fought well at Gettysburg, and but the year before had been assigned to the command of the Department of Tennessee.

—Frederick Douglass, quoted in *The Souls of Black Folk*,
by W. E. B. Du Bois

General Oliver Otis Howard (1830–1909)
Howard was a founding committee member and the third president of Howard University.
(Private collection)

Oliver Otis Howard, Civil War hero and founding member and third president of Howard University, was born to Rowland and Eliza Howard in Leeds, Maine, on November 8, 1830. Educated at Bowdoin College, he graduated from West Point Military Academy in 1854. With the outbreak of the Civil War, Howard, an opponent of slavery, entered the Union Army as Colonel of the Third Maine Volunteers.

Recognizing the sacrifice that must be made, Howard recalled, telling his family of his decision to join the Union Army, "Before entering my front gate, I raised my eyes and saw the picture of my little family framed in by the window. Home, family, comfort, beauty, joy, love were crowded into an instant of thought and feeling, as I sprang through the door and quickly ascended the stairway." All of the comforts of his home and life were placed at risk by his decision to join the Union Army. However, he was supported by a wife of equally strong convictions. And, as he would later recall, "My wife was patriotic, strong for the integrity of the Union, full of the heroic spirit, so when the crisis came, though so sudden and hard to bear, she said not one adverse word. I saw her watch me as I descended the slope toward the ferry landing, looked back, and waved my hat as I disappeared behind the ledge and trees."

Howard fought in the East from the first battle of Bull Run through the Gettysburg campaign, and lost his right arm at Fair Oaks. He also took part in battles at Antietam, Fredericksburg, Chancellorsville, and Gettysburg. After the death of J. B. Stewart, he commanded the Army of the Tennessee in Sherman's march through Atlanta.

The Civil War's end brought freedom to four million largely destitute former slaves. Recognizing their need for guidance and protection, Generals Grant and Sherman lobbied for an institution that could help. In March of 1865, Congress established the Bureau of Refugees, Freedmen and Abandoned Lands to assist newly emancipated slaves. In 1866, General Oliver Otis Howard, a deeply religious man, Civil War hero, and Medal of Honor recipient, was named its commissioner. General Howard believed that education would give the freedmen "both privileges and rights that we now have difficulty to guarantee." That same year the bureau's responsibilities and powers were expanded by Congress over President Andrew Johnson's veto.

In addition to providing former slaves with what many viewed as an equal education, the Freedmen's Bureau fought for their voting rights while enforcing their legal rights. As he was fighting these battles, Howard observed, "We then labored earnestly and unsuccessfully to elevate wages and defended the interest of the freedmen in their contracts, being constantly resisted by the inertia of the peculiar opinions of Southern property holders."

According to Howard, Secretary of War Edwin Stanton brought in a bushel basket heaped high with correspondence and, "with both hands holding the handles at each end, [he] took the basket and extended it to me and said: 'Here, General, *here's your Bureau!*'" Thus, began Gen-

William E. B. Du Bois (1868–1963)
A board member of Howard University, Du Bois was also a founder of the National Association for the Advancement of Colored People. A gifted sociologist, scholar, and author, he was a proponent of the "talented tenth" theory. (*Photograph courtesy Howard University Archives*)

eral Howard's commitment to developing a comprehensive education program for freedmen.

At that time there were two schools of thought regarding the educating of freedmen. Fisk and Atlanta Universities, among others, subscribed to the classical-curriculum school of thought, while Hampton, Tuskegee, and a number of others, known as normal or industrial schools, emphasized industrial and vocational training. It was believed that the latter approach quickly prepared former slaves to enter the job market, secure work, purchase land, and acquire businesses, while creating an economic base in their communities.

The radical differences between these two approaches fueled "the great debate between W.E.B. and Booker T." W.E.B. Du Bois, a Fisk University graduate, advocated advancement of the most "talented tenth" of the population through education in the arts and sciences. However, Booker T. Washington, a Hampton Normal School (now Hampton University) graduate, took a more generalist approach.

The classical-curriculum model was adopted for Howard, and a number of firsts followed. Howard, the oldest African-American comprehensive university, established the first medical teaching college for African-Americans. A law school and non-denominational theology department to teach the clergy followed.

In later years "Jim Crow" laws resulted in the harsh suppression of African-American rights. However, despite the great dangers they faced, schools like Howard University, Atlanta University, Wilberforce University, Hampton University, Morehouse College, Tuskegee University, and many others did not close their doors. Instead they continued to stand their ground and prepared for future battles by educating the premiere political and civil rights leaders.

BEVERAGES

Dean of Women's garden party for graduating senior women
(Photograph courtesy Howard University Archives)

Howard University School of Law

The Howard University School of Law enjoys a great tradition of producing lawyers committed to using the law creatively to seek social justice. This is a legacy to celebrate and build on as we make certain that our graduates are fully prepared to respond to the legal issues that will confront them both nationally and internationally.

—Kurt L. Schmoke, dean of Howard University School of Law

John Mercer Langston
Appointed dean of Howard University Law School in 1870, he was probably the first publicly elected African-American official in the U.S. *(Photograph courtesy Howard University Archives)*

Howard University School of Law, which originated as the Howard University Law Department, opened on January 6, 1869, with six students. In 1870, Professor John Mercer Langston was appointed dean.

In the early days, classes met three nights a week in the homes and offices of the four instructors. Eventually arrangements were made that permitted the department to use a room in the Second National Bank at 509 Seventh Street, N.W. At a later date, classes were held in the Lincoln Hall building on Ninth and D Street, N.W. When this building was destroyed by fire in 1886, classes were moved to Seventh and E Street, N.W.

Initially two years of study were required to receive an LL.B. degree. Of the ten two-year students who graduated on February 3, 1871, eight were admitted to practice in the District of Columbia on the following day.

Howard University law students in law library preparing a case
(Photograph courtesy Howard University Archives)

HOWARD HISTORY MAKER: John Mercer Langston, the first publicly elected African-American official in the United States, was twice suggested as a candidate for vice-president of the United States on the Republican ticket.

A house, located at 420 Fifth Street, N. W., and purchased by the University on June 23, 1887, served as the home of the law school until it moved to the main campus in 1936. Finally, in 1974, Dunbarton College at 2900 Van Ness Street, N.W., was purchased by the University, and it remains the home of the law school.

The untiring efforts of Dean Charles Hamilton Houston resulted in accreditation by the American Bar Association (ABA) in 1931. The law school's distinguished graduates and administrators include Thurgood Marshall (LL.B. 1933, first black United States Supreme Court Justice); Vernon E. Jordan, Jr., (LL.B. 1960, former president of the National Urban League); Damon Keith (LL.B. 1949, judge, United States Court of Appeals for the Sixth Circuit); William Bryant (LL.B. 1936, judge, United States District Court for the District of Columbia); Spottswood W. Robinson III (LL.B. 1939, chief judge, United States Court of Appeals for the District of Columbia); L. Douglas Wilder (former Governor of the State of Virginia); and Sharon Pratt Kelly (first woman mayor of the District of Columbia).

Created to provide legal education for African-Americans, Howard University leads the nation in educating civil rights attorneys dedicated to legally dismantling segregation. Graduates of the university engaged in groundbreaking civil rights litigation looked to their alma mater to provide the research and expert testimony upon which their arguments relied. Like foot soldiers during times of war, law students were drafted to the civil rights cause.

Harvard was training people to join big Wall Street firms. Howard was teaching lawyers to . . . go in court. And we used to hold fort in our little library . . . after school, at night and started to research problems. . . . Indeed, I remember . . . [one] guy, I believe it was Oliver Hill . . . found out that in codifying the code of the District of Columbia, they had just left out the Civil Rights Statute. . . . We eventually . . . got that straightened out. And we got to work on segregation.

—The Honorable Thurgood Marshall

In addition to producing an army of well-prepared and dedicated civil rights attorneys, the university assisted in preparing and presenting the Legal Defense Fund strategy. No other university provided this type and caliber of support to the war on segregation. The Howard Law School graduates and Dean Houston, among others, were on the front lines as they litigated many of the early cases challenging segregation in public education. Nine of the ten lawyers arguing *Brown v. Board of Education*, the landmark case declaring school segregation unconstitutional, were either graduates of or taught at Howard's law school. Among them was lead attorney Thurgood Marshall.

Thurgood Marshall: *American Revolutionary*

Born in Baltimore, Maryland, on July 2, 1908, Marshall, who graduated from high school at age sixteen, attended Lincoln University, the nation's oldest historically black college. Despite graduating from Lincoln with honors, Marshall was unable to attend the University of Maryland because he was an African-American. However, he was accepted at Howard University Law School, where he graduated first in the class of 1933.

Immediately after graduation Marshall entered private practice in Baltimore. Three years later he accepted a staff position offered by the National Association for the Advancement of Colored People (NAACP). From 1939 until 1961 he served as director and chief counsel for the organization's legal defense and education fund. In this position, he effectively removed barriers to racial equality by winning almost every precedent-setting case he argued before the Supreme Court. In deciding *Smith v. Allwright* in 1944, the Court struck down the "White Primary," a Texas practice aimed at excluding blacks from primary elections. In *Shelley v. Kraemer*, a 1948 case, Marshall persuaded the court to declare restrictive covenants preventing the sale of land to blacks unconstitutional and therefore unenforceable. *Sipuel v. University of Oklahoma*, argued in 1948, and *Sweatt v. Painter*, which followed in 1950, resulted in unanimous decisions from the court that forced the universities of Oklahoma and Texas to integrate their law schools.

However, Marshall's most precedent-setting argument before the Court came in 1954 when he argued *Brown v. Board of Education*.

Marshall argued that racial segregation in public schools violated the equal protection clause of the Fourteenth Amendment. In a unanimous decision the Court agreed. Overturning its previous decision in *Plessy v. Ferguson* (1889) the Court found that public school segregation was a violation of rights guaranteed by the Fourteenth Amendment to the Constitution.

Marshall achieved national recognition for his successful argument in this case and although he would win six additional cases in rapid succession that desegregated public parks, swimming pools, local bus systems, and athletic facilities, it was *Brown v. Board of Education* that broke ground for the civil rights protest work that followed in the 1950s and 60s.

Thurgood Marshall

A member of the Howard University class of 1933, Marshall successfully argued *Brown v. Board of Education* before the United States Supreme Court in 1954 and won more cases before the United States Supreme Court than any other American. In 1967 he became the first African-American to be appointed as an associate justice of the U.S. Supreme Court, where he served until his retirement in 1991. A valiant and skilled warrior on the field of legal battle, Thurgood Marshall died in 1993.
(Photograph courtesy Howard University Archives)

CHERRY LEMONADE

Try this delightfully refreshing lemonade on a hot summer day, and experience the sweet fragrance of cherry blossoms wafting on a cool breeze!

4   cups pitted, fresh, sweet
      cherries, coarsely chopped
¾   cup water
2   cups sugar
2   cups fresh lemon juice

5½   cups water
2   drops red food coloring (optional)
4   cups fresh sweet cherries, halved
      and pitted

Place 4 cups cherries in saucepan with ¾ cup water and bring to a quick boil. Reduce heat and simmer 7 minutes, or until the cherries are soft. Strain the mixture through a sieve, pressing it through with the back of a spoon to extract as much juice as possible. Return juice to the saucepan, add sugar, and bring to a boil; reduce heat and simmer 5 minutes or until the mixture becomes syrupy. Cool and transfer syrup to a serving pitcher, add remaining ingredients, mix well, and adjust sugar and water to taste. Serve in tall, chilled, ice-filled glasses.

8 servings

Kenneth B. Clark and Mamie Phipps Clark

American social psychologists Kenneth and Mamie Phipps Clark are best known for their highly regarded research on the social and psychological effects of racism and segregation on schoolchildren.

After graduating from high school in Harlem, New York, Kenneth Clark entered Howard University, where he earned a bachelor's degree and was working on his master's when he met Mamie Phipps, his future wife and lifelong collaborator and colleague. A sixteen-year-old-freshman when she arrived on Howard's campus in the fall of 1934, Mamie was the daughter of Dr. Harold and Kate Florence Phipps. In addition to a private medical practice, Dr. Phipps owned and operated a hotel and spa for black patrons.

As a result of her family's social and financial standing in her native Hot Springs, Arkansas, Mamie led a life somewhat sheltered from the harsh realities of racism. When it was time for her to travel east to college, her father reserved a compartment on the train for her, in order to "protect her from racial incidents during the trip." Ironically, the most important work of Mamie's life would involve proving the harmful psychological and social effects of unequal race-based treatment upon children. It would later form the basis of one of the legal arguments used by Thurgood Marshall and the eight other Howard University Law School graduates and professors who were part of the legal team attacking school segregation in *Brown v. Board of Education.*

Kenneth was a graduate student and teaching assistant in Howard's psychology department when the two met. They began a relationship that continued throughout most of Mamie's undergraduate years. In the summer of 1937, Mamie's junior year, Kenneth Clark was accepted to Columbia University as its first black graduate student.

The couple wrote to each other daily and visited whenever they could. At the end of one such visit, Mamie wrote, "Really, Kenneth, I am happier than I ever dared imagine. Those two days with you were like a grand holiday where you just revel in deliciousness. . . . All of it was so very nice—you'll never know what it meant to me." Unable to wait any longer to be together, they were engaged in the fall of 1937, over the objections of Mamie's parents. Fearful that an early marriage would interrupt her education and ruin her future, her father wrote a letter to Mamie in which he protested that he "had envisaged an entirely different programme for you; a brilliant scholastic career; equal brilliance in your chosen field of endeavor, then for me the honor and pleasure of giving you away in marriage. Such a course would have capped off the interest and pride I have always had in. . . . you. But all of these hopes have been dashed to pieces."

Nevertheless, in the spring of 1938, a few months prior to Mamie's graduation, the couple, very much in love, secretly eloped. Kenneth would later reflect that Mamie "had already been elected May Queen, which meant she was virginal. And we didn't want to mess up the May Queen affair. So we kept our marriage secret—except for my parents." In addition, revelation of the marriage would have resulted in Mamie's expulsion from school because undergraduate students were not permitted to marry.

In 1938 Mamie graduated magna cum laude and that summer she accepted a law office position with William Houston, who was instrumental in the early planning of civil rights cases. Houston's family was well known in education, law, and medicine. His brother, Ulysses L. Houston, was the first Chief of the Division of Otolaryngology at Howard University Hospital, and his nephew, Charles L. Houston, architect of the National Association for the Advancement of Colored People (NAACP) Civil Rights Legal Defense program, was dean of Howard's law school.

The studies of the long-term effects of racism on Washington, D.C., schoolchildren begun by Mamie and Kenneth while they were at Howard led to their classic 1939 study in which they found that African-American preschoolers preferred white dolls to

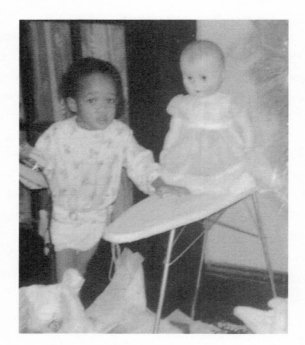

Child with doll
Private collection

black ones. In 1950 the Clarks prepared a report on the problems of minority youth for the White House Mid-Century Conference on Youth, later published in revised form as *Prejudice and Your Child* (1955), which summarized the results of the doll tests and related research and attracted the attention of the NAACP as it was preparing to challenge the laws requiring segregation in the nation's schools.

The Clarks' work for the NAACP played a major role in the Supreme Court's 1954 decision in *Brown v. Board of Education*. In a unanimous opinion, Chief Justice Earl Warren wrote ". . . the policy of separating the races is usually interpreted as denoting the inferiority of the Negro group. A sense of inferiority affects the motivation of the child to learn. Segregation with the sanction of law, therefore, has a tendency to retard the educational and mental development of Negro children. . . ." The first social study cited by Chief Justice Warren in support of the Court's finding was *The Effects of Prejudice and Discrimination on Personality Development* by Kenneth and Mamie Clark.

PEACH LEMONADE

3 peaches, peeled, pitted, and coarsely chopped	4 cups water
1 cup sugar	1 cup fresh lemon juice
	Fresh mint for garnish

Bring peaches, sugar, and water to a boil. Reduce heat and simmer until sugar dissolves, approximately 5 minutes. Strain the peach mixture through a sieve, pressing through to extract as much juice as possible. Cool syrup and transfer to a serving pitcher. Add lemon juice to the syrup, mix well, and refrigerate for at least an hour before serving. Serve in tall, chilled, ice-filled glasses. Garnish with a sprig of mint.

4 to 6 servings

WATERMELON LEMONADE

Watermelon is so versatile that there are a number of ways to enjoy it. The Tillery household discovered most of them and particularly loved the delectable lemonade. I hope you enjoy it as much as we did!

8 cups watermelon, cubed and seeded	½ cup sugar
½ cup raspberries	¾ cup fresh lemon juice
¼ cup water	¼ cup pineapple juice

Process the watermelon, raspberries, and water in a food processor until they are blended smooth. Strain the mixture through a fine mesh strainer into a serving pitcher. Stir in sugar, lemon juice, and pineapple juice until sugar dissolves. Refrigerate until thoroughly chilled, approximately 1 hour. Serve in tall, chilled, ice-filled glasses.

4 to 6 servings

RASPBERRY LEMONADE WITH RASPBERRY ICE CUBES

¾	cup fresh raspberries	1¼	teaspoons fresh mint, minced
1¼	cups fresh lemon juice	6	cups water
1	cup granulated sugar		

Purée raspberries and strain juice into a serving pitcher by placing purée in a fine mesh strainer and pressing with the back of a spoon. Discard pulp and add remaining ingredients; mix well. Adjust sugar and water to taste and serve in tall, chilled, "raspberry" ice-filled glasses. (See recipe on page 23.)

6 servings

Charlotte Ray

When Charlotte Ray was admitted to the Howard University School of Law in 1870, she became the second woman to attend an organized law school in the United States. Upon graduating in 1872, Ray, the daughter of a well-known abolitionist and conductor on the Underground Railroad, became not only the first African-American female lawyer, but also the first woman admitted to the District of Columbia Bar Association. Shortly thereafter, she entered private practice, and it was not long before the press took note of her.

In the city of Washington, where a few years ago colored women were bought and sold under sanction of law, a woman of African-American descent has been admitted to practice law at the Supreme Court of the District of Columbia. Miss Charlotte E. Ray, who has the honor of being the first lady lawyer in Washington, is a graduate of the Law College of Howard University, and is said to be possessing quite an intelligent countenance. She doubtlessly has a fine mind and deserves success.

—Women's Journal, 1872

Despite an earlier presentation on Chancery that earned her recognition as one of the most astute young legal minds in the country, gender and race bias forced Charlotte Ray to close her practice. During the Margaret Brent Award ceremony on August 5, 2001 (the award honors the accomplishments of women lawyers who have excelled in their field and paved the way for other women lawyers) Charlotte Ray was remembered by Howard alumna Gabrielle McDonald, a former federal judge and international criminal tribunal justice. Judge McDonald remarked, "In 1872, she would not have been eligible to receive this award. Today 129 years later, I accept this award and do so in honor of Charlotte Ray. . . . Let's not permit another Charlotte E. Ray to be lost from our profession. . . ."

RASPBERRY ICE CUBES

Your guests will be delighted as the ice cubes melt and the ruby jewels hidden within them yield their sweet surprise!

1	cup granulated sugar	1	tablespoon fresh lemon juice
½	cup water	1	cup fresh raspberries

Combine sugar and water in a saucepan and bring to a quick boil over medium-high heat. Reduce heat and simmer for 10 minutes. Remove the pan from heat and cool contents to room temperature before stirring in the lemon juice and raspberries. Spoon cooled mixture into ice cube trays and freeze solid. Place frozen raspberry cubes in tall glasses and pour raspberry lemonade over them.

4 servings

Charles Hamilton "Charlie" Houston

We stand on the shoulders of Howard's Charles Hamilton Houston. He made the law school a civil rights citadel where lawyers like Thurgood Marshall, Vernon Jordan, and President James Madison Nabrit Jr. were trained to battle for justice; and all Americans became heirs to laws that can, in the words of the prophet Amos, allow "justice to roll down like waters and righteousness like a mighty stream."

—WILLIAM E. KENNARD,
Chairman, Federal Communications Commission,
Commencement Exercises, May 13, 2000

Charles Hamilton Houston

The first African-American editor of the *Harvard Law Review* and dean of Howard University's Law School from 1930 to 1935, Houston was the chief architect of the strategy in *Brown v. Board of Education*. Although he died in 1950, four years before the *Brown* decision was reached, he continues to be celebrated as "the man who killed Jim Crow." *(Photograph courtesy Howard University Archives)*

Civil rights attorney Charles Houston, a staunch opponent of segregation and a legal visionary, was born in Washington, D.C., on September 3, 1895, just blocks from the United States Supreme Court Building. Mary Hamilton Houston, a black hairdresser and wife of William Houston, a general practice attorney, gave birth to a child who would one day lead a legal attack that would reshape race relations in America.

Almost from birth, Houston's future was shaped by the legal events of his time. One such event was the case of *Plessy v. Ferguson*, which the Court heard one month after Houston's birth. Houston would one day be instrumental in dismantling *Plessy*, which would sound the death knell for the principle of "separate but equal."

In 1892, Homer Adolf Plessy, who was one-eighth black, purchased a ticket from New Orleans to Covington and sat in the "white" section of the East Louisiana Railroad Company train. After receiving an earlier tip that Plessy, who appeared white, was in fact black, railroad officials confronted him. Upon his refusal to sit in the "colored" car, Plessy was forcibly ejected from the train and later charged with violating Louisiana's recently enacted law that separated the races. In October of 1895, after Plessy argued that Louisiana's law violated the Fourteenth Amendment's guarantee of equal protection under the law, the U.S. Supreme Court upheld the state's "Separate Car Law."

The Court's decision gave rise to the legal principle of "separate but equal," which would guide American race relations for over half a century. The "separate" facilities referenced in the decision were either nonexistent or so inferior that they could not be considered equal, and as a result of *Plessy*, African-American citizens were robbed of the rights granted to them under the Fourteenth and Fifteenth Amendments. In many respects this decision was akin to returning African-Americans to the legal uncertainties of slavery.

As another result of *Plessy*, Charles Hamilton Houston came of age in a legally segregated district. At age twelve, he entered M Street High School (later known as Dunbar High School). The first all-black high school in the United States, M Street was remarkable in that it offered a traditional classical curriculum. At that time, most secondary black schools offered either a vocational or "general" curriculum. After graduating from high school, Houston received a partial scholarship to study at Amherst College. Upon graduating in June of 1915, he returned to Washington, D.C., and taught English and "Negro Literature" at Howard.

When the United States entered World War I in 1917, Charles secured a position at the first black officers' training camp in Fort Des Moines, Iowa, where black officers were segregated from their white counterparts. In later years, Houston would recall, "special latrines and showers [were] boarded off so we [officers] would not physically come in contact with white enlisted men."

Moreover, they were not permitted to eat in the officer's mess, but were instead required to eat on benches in the enlisted men's area. And although 40 percent of black men assigned to Fort Des Moines were college graduates, the racist camp commander asserted they lacked the "mental potential and higher qualities of character essential to command and leadership." After experiencing race-based abuse and witnessing the harassment of other black soldiers, Houston resolved to "never get caught again without knowing my rights; that if luck was with me, and I got through this war, I would study law and use my time fighting for men who could not strike back."

In February 1919, while traveling aboard a train, Houston and another black officer sat next to a middle-aged white southerner who immediately demanded their removal. Within two months of that encounter, Charles Houston left the army, declaring, "My battleground is in America, not France."

During the summer of 1919, Houston observed what he called "the greatest period of interracial strife the nation had ever witnessed." During that summer, a twenty-five-year-old black man shot and killed a white Marine while defending himself from an angry mob. Houston's father tried the case and, despite clear evidence supporting his claim of self-defense, an all-white jury convicted the man. That fall Houston applied for admission to Harvard Law School. An exceptional student, his academic performance earned him a position on the editorial board of the *Harvard Law Review*. He was the first African-American to earn such an honor. After graduating in the top 5 percent of his class, he began graduate studies that would lead to a doctorate in juridical science.

Recognizing the need for black law professors, Houston applied for a teaching position at Howard Law School, which since its establishment in 1869 had trained three-fourths of the black lawyers in the United States. In a letter of recommendation, Dean Roscoe Pound assured Howard that Houston "gives promise of becoming a real legal scholar." Professor Charles Houston's first assignment was to teach "Agency," "Surety and Mortgages," "Jurisprudence," and "Administrative Law" to first- and second-year law students at Howard.

[The] only justification for Howard Law School . . . is necessary
work for the social good.
—Charles Hamilton Houston

By 1927, Houston was firmly focused on the issue of racial equality, and in the 1930s he began filing precedent-setting cases that targeted segregation in public schools. His rising reputation attracted many promising students to the school, including Thurgood Marshall. Houston was a tough professor. Marshall later recalled, "Charlie Houston . . . gave an examination in evidence in our second year that started at nine o'clock in the morning and ended at five in the afternoon. One subject."

Houston continued to attract the attentions of civil rights activists and soon NAACP Executive Secretary Walter White called on him to serve on its National Legal Committee. In October 1934, Houston recommended that the NAACP launch a concentrated legal attack against segregated public education. The NAACP was impressed and appointed Houston special counsel. Shortly thereafter, he boarded a train in Washington and traveled to the NAACP national offices in New York and began the long walk toward dismantling *Plessy*. A number of successes followed. However, four years before *Brown v. Board of Education Topeka* was decided, Houston passed away. The mantle was passed to his protégé, Thurgood Marshall.

A lawyer's either a social engineer or . . . a parasite on society. . . . A social engineer [is] a highly skilled, perceptive, sensitive lawyer who [understands] the Constitution of the United States and [knows] how to explore its uses in the solving of problems of local communities and in bettering conditions of the underprivileged citizens.

—Charles Hamilton Houston

Sparkling Strawberry-Mint Lemonade

1	quart fresh strawberries, hulled		3	cups cold water
1	cup fresh lemon juice		½	cup sugar
2¼	cups chilled lemon-lime soda			Mint syrup *(see recipe on page 28)*

Purée strawberries and remove to a serving pitcher. Add the remaining ingredients and mix well. Adjust sugar and soda to taste and serve in tall, chilled, ice-filled glasses.

6 to 8 servings

M I N T   S Y R U P

This tasty mint syrup is also delicious in iced tea.

2½ cups water	1 cup mint leaves (approximately
1 cup sugar	¾ ounce)

Bring water and sugar to a quick boil and stir until sugar dissolves. Remove saucepan from the heat and gently stir in the mint leaves. Cover saucepan and allow mint to steep for 30 minutes or until leaves are sufficiently cool to handle. Squeeze liquid from leaves back into steeping pot and discard leaves. Transfer syrup to a screw-top jar or other tight-lidded container. Refrigerate.

Yields approximately 2 cups

Watermelon Margaritas

Watermelons are no longer just for eating. I am sure you will agree that this mouthwatering margarita makes excellent use of this delicious and versatile melon.

Lime juice	⅓ cup baker's sugar
Baker's sugar or other fine granulated sugar	2 tablespoons vodka
½ cup tequila	2 tablespoons pineapple juice
2¾ cups seeded, chopped watermelon	

Rub rims of 4 margarita glasses with lime juice and immediately dip in sugar, set glasses aside for sugar to dry. Combine remaining ingredients in a food processor and process smooth before serving in prepared glasses. May be made up to 1 month in advance and stored in zippered, plastic storage bags in the freezer.

4 servings

Set your goals carefully and fearlessly and pursue them unswervingly.
—Spottswood Robinson

Spottswood W. Robinson III *(right)* was the grandson of a former slave. Robinson greatly admired and was strongly influenced by his grandfather, who overcame social obstacles to become a successful businessman. A 1939 magna cum laude graduate of Howard University School of Law, Robinson taught at the school until 1947, when he left to enter private practice. From 1948 until 1960 he served as a lawyer for the NAACP Legal Defense Fund. In this position he was involved in numerous federal cases, including *Davis v. County School Board of Prince Edward County,* one of the cases considered by the Supreme Court along with *Brown v. Board of Education.* His brilliantly fought cases gave all Americans equal rights

- to purchase property
- to travel on public transportation
- to public education
- to use public recreational facilities

In 1960 Robinson returned to Howard to become dean of the law school, and he served as a member of the United States Commission on Civil Rights from 1961 to 1963. Following his 1966 appointment by President Lyndon Baines Johnson, Robinson became the first African-American to sit on the U.S. Court of Appeals for the District of Columbia. In 1981 he achieved another African-American first when he was named as the Chief Judge of the court. *(Private collection)*

SPICED CRANBERRY APPLE JUICE

3	cups cranberry juice		⅔	cup orange juice
2	cups apple juice		½	cup fresh lemon juice
6	whole cloves		3	tablespoons fresh lime juice
2	2-inch cinnamon sticks			

Combine the first 4 ingredients in a saucepan and bring to a quick boil, reduce heat and simmer 5 to 7 minutes. Allow the mixture to cool, stir in citrus juices, and chill before transferring to a serving pitcher and pouring into tall, chilled, ice-filled glasses.

6 servings

George E. C. Hayes

George E. C. Hayes, born in Richmond, Virginia, in 1894, was part of the original "Dream Team" of lawyers, who dismantled *Plessy* and put an end to mandatory racial segregation. Like Charles Hamilton Houston, Hayes was a graduate of M Street High School in Washington, D.C. He received his undergraduate degree from Brown University.

Following in the footsteps of his father, attorney James H. Hayes, George became a lawyer, completing his law degree at Howard University in 1918. In 1924, he joined the faculty and was appointed the university's first legal advisor in 1937. During this period the law school faculty and students began developing a legal response to the social injustices confronting African-Americans. Hayes worked for four years without fee on *Bolling v. Sharpe*. (*Bolling* was one of four cases the Court would hear in deciding *Brown v. Board of Education Topeka*.)

Communism was the issue when Hayes took on Senator Joseph McCarthy in March of 1954 in a case involving forty-nine-year-old Annie Lee Moss. Moss, a civilian employee of the U.S. Army Signal Corps in Washington, D.C., had lost her job after McCarthy accused her of Communist Party membership and espionage. Following an appearance before the House Un-American Activities Committee, she was cleared. The white press, in a surprising reaction, equated HUAC tactics with a public lynching and noted "the humiliating defeat McCarthy brought on himself in the Annie Lee Moss case, which [was defended by] an able Negro lawyer, George E. C. Hayes of Washington."

In February of 1955, President Dwight Eisenhower appointed Howard graduate E. C. Hayes to the Public Utilities Commission of the District of Columbia, making him the highest-ranking African-American in D.C. government.

AMBER TEA

This tawny tea is as smooth as liquid gold and delightfully refreshing!

4	cups boiling water	3	cups fresh orange juice
8	teabags	1½	cups apricot nectar
1	cup sugar	3	quarts chilled ginger ale
1	cup fresh lemon juice		

Pour boiling water over teabags and steep for 5 minutes. Remove and discard teabags. Combine tea with remaining ingredients, except ginger ale. Refrigerate to chill through and add ginger ale just prior to serving in tall, chilled, ice-filled glasses.

24 servings

TROPICAL MINT TEA

7	cups boiling water	1	cup sugar
7	teabags	½	cup fresh lemon juice
15	sprigs fresh mint	¼	cup fresh orange juice

Pour boiling water over teabags and mint; steep 5 minutes. Remove and discard teabags and mint. Add sugar to the infused tea and stir until it dissolves. Allow tea mixture to cool before pouring it into a serving pitcher. Combine brewed tea with lemon and orange juices, mix well, and refrigerate 1 hour before serving in tall, chilled, ice-filled glasses.

6 to 8 servings

ORANGE-MINT TEA

Cool, refreshing mint adds zing to this scrumptious orange tea!

2¼	cups sugar	6	cups brewed tea (double strength)
¾	cup water	6	cups fresh orange juice
7	sprigs fresh mint		

Bring sugar and water to a boil, reduce heat to low, and stir until sugar completely dissolves. Remove mixture from heat, bruise mint leaves, and add to the sugar mixture. Cover pot and steep approximately 30 minutes. Remove and discard mint leaves.

Combine sugar mixture, brewed tea, and orange juice in a serving pitcher. Mix well and adjust sugar to taste. Chill thoroughly before serving in tall, chilled, ice-filled glasses.

10 to 12 servings

RASPBERRY AND MINT TEA WITH RASPBERRY ICE CUBES

1	pint fresh raspberries	2	cups sugar
4	cups chilled tea	1¼	teaspoons fresh mint, minced
¼	cup fresh lemon juice		Raspberries to garnish

Purée raspberries and strain juice into a serving pitcher by placing pulp in a fine mesh strainer and pressing with the back of a spoon, to extract as much juice as possible. Add the remaining ingredients to the pitcher and stir until the sugar dissolves. Adjust sugar and water to taste and serve in tall, chilled, raspberry ice cube-filled glasses (see recipe on page 23). Garnish with raspberries.

4 servings

CITRUS ISLAND TEA

3   cups water
5   whole cloves
1   family-size teabag
1   cup sugar
1¾   cups pineapple juice

¾   cup orange juice
¼   cup fresh lime juice
     Fresh mint sprigs
     Orange slices

Bring the water and cloves to a boil over medium-high heat, reduce heat, and simmer 10 minutes. Remove saucepan from heat, add the teabag, and steep for 10 minutes. Remove and discard teabag and cloves. Add sugar and stir until sugar dissolves. Add the fruit juices and mix well. Add additional sugar to taste and chill before serving in tall, chilled, ice-filled glasses. Garnish with mint sprigs and orange slices.

6 servings

HONEY AND CITRUS TEA PUNCH

9   cups freshly brewed, orange
     spice tea (double strength)
2   cups honey
¾   cup pineapple juice

¾   cup fresh orange juice
¼   cup plus 2 tablespoons fresh lemon
     juice
1   quart lemon-lime soda

Combine tea, honey, and juices. Stir until honey is thoroughly blended, and chill. Add lemon-lime soda just before serving and pour into a punch bowl over a block of ice.

20 to 24 punch cup servings

Punch Notes: When making punch, double your recipe and freeze half in a ring form or tube cake pan. Substitute the frozen punch block for ice. In this way, your punch is never watered down by melting ice; and the punch bowl becomes self-replenishing.

TROPICAL FRUIT AND WATERMELON PUNCH

5	cups water	1	large sweet watermelon
1⅓	cups fresh lime juice	4	cups fresh strawberries, washed, cored, and quartered
4	cups fresh orange juice		
2	cups sugar		

Bring first four ingredients to a boil in a saucepan. Boil 3 minutes. Allow mixture to cool. Remove watermelon from the shell and seed and cube the watermelon flesh. Combine cooled juice mixture, watermelon, and strawberries in a food processor and process until blended smooth. Strain the pureed mixture through a fine mesh strainer into serving pitchers. Discard pulp. Refrigerate until chilled through, approximately 1 hour. Pour over a block of ice into a punch bowl.

24 servings

RHUBARB PUNCH

2	pounds fresh rhubarb, diced	1	cup fresh lemon juice
4	cups water	½	cup lime juice
2	sprigs fresh mint	6	cups cold water
1½	cups sugar		Fresh mint
3½	cups fresh orange juice		

Bring first two ingredients to a boil, reduce heat, and simmer until rhubarb is fork tender, approximately 30 to 45 minutes. Add mint and sugar and stir until the sugar dissolves. Allow mixture to cool. Remove and discard mint. Strain the mixture through a coarse sieve, pressing through, using the back of a spoon to extract as much juice as possible. Add the remaining ingredients, mix well, and pour over a block of ice into a punch bowl. Garnish with sprigs of fresh mint.

20 to 24 servings

Ollie Mae Cooper

Revered by many of Howard University's alumni, Ollie May Cooper was the first black woman to be admitted by examination to the bar of the District of Columbia. Born in 1887 in Tennessee, she moved with her family to the District of Columbia when she was a child. She attended public school there and received her law degree from Howard University in 1921. She was admitted to the bar on October 11, 1926.

A role model for all and an early pioneer for black women in the law, Cooper broke barriers while practicing law in the District of Columbia. She and Isadora Lecher were the first black women to open a law firm in the United States. Ollie May Cooper was also the first black woman to be admitted to the appeals court of the District of Columbia and to hold a national office in the National Bar Association. In addition, she was a founder of Epsilon Sigma Iota, a legal sorority for black women.

CLASS REUNION: TROPICAL LEMONADE PUNCH FOR FIFTY

2	pounds sugar	1	16-ounce can diced pineapples
	juice from 25 lemons	2	gallons water
	juice from 12 oranges	2	cups maraschino cherries with juice
6	oranges, sliced		

Combine sugar with the fruit juice and bring to a quick boil. Remove from heat and cool. Add remaining ingredients and mix well. Pour over a block of ice into a punch bowl.

50 servings

ROSEMARY PINEAPPLEADE PUNCH

8½ cups pineapple juice, divided	¼ cup sugar
3½ teaspoons fresh rosemary leaves (stems removed)	¾ cup fresh lemon juice
	¼ cup fresh lime juice

Bring ½ cup of the pineapple juice and rosemary leaves to a boil. Remove from heat, cover and steep 10 minutes. Strain leaves from the juice and combine infused juice with the remaining ingredients. Pour into a punch bowl over a block of ice.

20 to 24 servings

HOT SPICED ORANGE TEA

1 quart water	¼ cup fresh orange juice
¼ cup sugar	2 tablespoons fresh lemon juice
12 whole cloves	1 tablespoon fresh lime juice
3 2-inch cinnamon sticks	Rind of ¼ of a medium orange
4 teabags	Orange wedges to garnish

Bring the first four ingredients to a boil. Stir to mix well. Remove from heat, add teabags and steep 7 minutes. During last minute of steeping add juices and orange rind. Strain the tea into a warmed teapot or individual serving cups. Garnish with orange or lemon wedge.

6 servings

HOT SPICED CIDER

2 tablespoons whole cloves	6 cinnamon sticks
2 tablespoons whole allspice	1 cup sugar
1 bay leaf	36 ounces apple juice
4 cups water	

Place first three ingredients in a muslin or gauze "spice" bag. In a large saucepan, bring water to a quick boil. Add spice bag, cinnamon sticks, and sugar, reduce heat and simmer 15 minutes. Add apple juice and simmer an additional 15 minutes. Serve hot in individual mugs.

8 to 10 servings

CREAMY HOT SPICED CHOCOLATE

Although many years have passed since my mother served this drink when I came in from snow play, it remains one of my favorites. When we are in the North I eagerly anticipate the first flake of snow.

4 cups half-and-half	9 squares (9 ounces) semisweet chocolate
3 cups milk	Heavy cream, whipped
½ teaspoon ground cinnamon	Nutmeg
¼ teaspoon ground nutmeg	

Combine half-and-half, milk, cinnamon, and nutmeg in a 2½-quart saucepan. Bring mixture to a simmer over low heat, but do not boil. Add chocolate and stir. When chocolate melts, remove saucepan from heat and mix well. Pour into individual mugs and serve piping hot, topped with whipped cream and a dash of nutmeg.

6 to 7 servings

Winter at Howard University
(Photograph courtesy Howard University Archives)

HINT OF MINT HOT CHOCOLATE

Chase away the chill of winter with a sip of this delicious hot chocolate. Smile as you remember when you and your dormmates did the same.

4   cups half-and-half
3   cups milk
¼   teaspoon ground cinnamon
9   squares (9 ounces) semisweet
      chocolate

1   tablespoon crème de menthe
    Whipped cream for garnish

Combine half-and-half, milk, and cinnamon in a 2½-quart saucepan. Bring mixture to a simmer over low heat, but do not boil. Add chocolate and stir. When chocolate melts, remove saucepan from heat, gently blend in crème de menthe. Pour into individual mugs, top with whipped cream, and serve piping hot.

6 to 7 servings

CAFÉ AU CHOCOLATE

This wonderfully rich blend of coffee and chocolate is guaranteed to satisfy the child in you while allowing you to maintain your adult dignity.

4   cups half-and-half
3   cups milk
½   teaspoon ground cinnamon
9   squares (9 ounces) semisweet
      chocolate

2   tablespoons butter
¼   teaspoon nutmeg
1   cup strong hot coffee
    Heavy cream, whipped

Combine half-and-half, milk, and cinnamon in a 2½-quart saucepan. Bring mixture to a simmer over low heat, but do not boil. Add chocolate and butter; stir. When chocolate and butter melt, remove the saucepan from heat and add the nutmeg and hot coffee. Pour into individual mugs, top with whipped cream, and serve piping hot.

4 to 6 servings

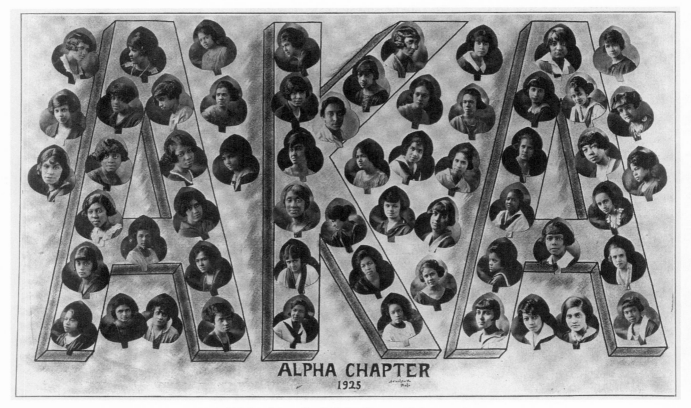

"Alpha chapter" of Alpha Kappa Alpha sorority
The oldest Greek-letter organization established by and for African-American college women, Alpha Kappa Alpha was founded on the campus of Howard University by Ethel Hedgeman Lyle on January 15, 1908. *(Photograph courtesy Howard University Archives)*

BOURBON AND CREAM EGGNOG

1	quart milk		2	cups bourbon
1	pint heavy cream		2	tablespoons vanilla extract
12	eggs		½	teaspoon ground nutmeg, divided
½	teaspoon salt		2	cups French vanilla ice cream
1¾	cups sugar		1	quart whipping cream

In a large saucepan, combine milk and heavy cream; bring this milk mixture to a simmer over medium heat, but *do not* boil. Beat eggs with an electric beater until well blended and pale yellow in color. Combine salt and sugar before adding the salt mixture to the eggs a little at a time, beating well after each addition. Next, slowly stir approximately one-fourth of the hot milk into the egg mixture. Mix well, then add remainder of the milk. Continue to cook over medium-low heat, stirring constantly, for 25 to 30 minutes or until the mixture reaches 160 degrees, thickens, and can coat the back of a spoon. Stir in bourbon, vanilla extract, ¼ teaspoon nutmeg, and ice cream. Remove from heat, cover, and chill. The eggnog may be made to this point up to two days in advance. Place in a punch bowl and immediately before serving, beat whipping cream at medium speed until soft peaks form. Fold whipped cream into eggnog. Sprinkle with remaining nutmeg.

12 to 16 servings

WASHINGTON PUNCH

2¼ cups diced pineapple	Large block of ice
1¼ cups sugar	2 cups pineapple slices
¾ bottle Moselle wine	1 cup maraschino cherries, with juice
2 bottles Rhine wine	1 quart domestic champagne
1 cup pineapple juice	

Sprinkle the diced pineapple with the sugar and add the Moselle wine; cover loosely with plastic wrap, and allow to stand undisturbed for 24 hours. Strain mixture, discard the pineapple, and add Rhine wine to the strained liquid. Add the pineapple juice and mix well. Pour punch into a large punch bowl over the ice block. Add the pineapple slices and the maraschino cherries. Stir in the champagne immediately before serving, and enjoy!

20 servings

Law students at Howard University
(Photograph courtesy Howard University Archives)

Howard's law students and an army of her graduate lawyers tirelessly fought on the legal front to challenge discriminatory laws that violated the constitutional rights of African-American citizens. However, when states were slow to enact hard-won legal decisions, Howard students fought on another, equally important front.

At the forefront of the student protest movement, Howard students could be found organizing, protesting, and giving voice to the cause. Despite abuse, beatings, jail, and threats to their lives, they continued the fight in the tradition of General O. O. Howard and others who went before them. In the end it was litigation *and* demonstration that led to the signing of the Civil Rights Act of 1964 and the Voting Rights Act of 1965.

Mrs. Medgar Evers at a protest rally
(Corbis)

APPETIZERS

Student Protest

. . . We come then to the question presented: Does segregation of children in public schools solely on the basis of race, even though the physical facilities and other "tangible" factors may be equal, deprive the children of the minority group of equal education opportunities? We believe that it does. . . . We conclude that in the field of public education the doctrine of "separate but equal" has no place. Separate educational facilities are inherently unequal. . . .

—Chief Justice Earl Warren, reading the unanimous decision of the Court
in *Brown v. Board of Education,* May 17, 1954

While the Supreme Court's decision in *Brown v. Board of Education* ended legally mandated segregation of public schools in the United States, it did not specify a date by which schools were to be desegregated. And it was equally silent with regard to segregation of public facilities such as restaurants, restrooms, and transportation accommodations on public highways.

Frustrated and angered by the slow response of states to the decision, their otherwise unequal treatment, and continued voting rights violations, African-Americans initiated a grass roots protest movement, which began in the late 1950s. Students, who often spearheaded the protests, influenced some of the most revolutionary breakthroughs in equal-rights legislation since the Reconstruction period. Leading the way, as always, were Howard University students and faculty.

For many African-Americans, it was in the fiery cauldron of the Civil Rights Movement that character and leadership abilities were forged and refined. Many outstanding individuals who awakened the conscience of America and led ordinary people—domestic workers, students, farmers—to take extraordinary actions in the cause of equality and freedom, were taught their skills in wide-reaching organizations such as SCLC, CORE, and SNCC.

—James H. Johnson, Dean, College of Engineering, Architecture, and Computer Sciences
SECME Conference—Howard University, July 11, 2002

Following the *Brown* decision, protest placed pressure on the government to end all legally sanctioned segregation of public facilities in the United States. However, segregationists resisted, especially in southern states where as late as 1960, several schools ignored the decision in *Brown* and refused to integrate.

In addition, the Ku Klux Klan continued enforcing "Jim Crow" segregation through a systematic pattern of terrorism and intimidation. Fearless in the face of mounting danger, student protesters brought the inequities of the system into the living rooms of ordinary, middle-class Americans who, for the most part, had remained silent on the issue. Howard students were key to the success of this new phase of the civil rights movement. Almost two decades earlier, Howard University students James Farmer and Anna Pauli Murray laid the foundation for the movement's successful nonviolent strategy.

James Farmer

The fight for freedom is combined with the fight for equality, and we must realize that this is the fight for America—not just black America but all America. In the words of the great rabbi who wrote, 2,000 years ago, "Hither, if I am not for myself, who will be for me; if I am for myself alone, what am I? If not now, when?"

—James Farmer,
Central State College Speech,
Wilberforce, Ohio, October 26, 1964

Civil rights legend James Farmer, a founder of the Congress of Racial Equality, which shaped the U.S. civil rights struggle in the mid-1950s and 60s, was born in Marshall, Texas, on January 12, 1920. The son of a minister and grandson of a slave, Farmer was a follower of Mohandas Gandhi, and applied Gandhi's principles in adopting a strategy of nonviolent student protest in the United States. This strategy became a most effective weapon in the movement's war against racism.

Farmer was an outstanding student, earning a bachelor of science degree from Wiley College (1938) and a bachelor of divinity from Howard in 1941. In 1942, at age 22, he helped to organize the Congress of Racial Equality (CORE), which pioneered nonviolent protest in the United States as a means of directly challenging racism.

Farmer's nonviolent strategies were often met with violence, however, and he routinely risked his life for the cause of integration. He narrowly avoided death during a 1963 incident in which armed Louisiana state troopers hunted him door to door after he attempted to organize the town of Plaquemine. "I was meant to die that night," Farmer later recalled. "They were kicking open doors, beating up blacks in the streets, interrogating them with electric cattle prods." He credits his escape to a quick-thinking funeral home director who ordered Farmer to "play dead" and carried him out of town in the back of a hearse.

In 1961, Farmer became national director of CORE and was instrumental in organizing the campaign of student sit-ins and Freedom Rides that broke the back of southern segregation and discrimination. The CORE-sponsored Freedom Rides challenged segregated accommodations in interstate

Civil rights legend James Farmer, founder of the Congress of Racial Equality (CORE)
(Photograph courtesy Howard University Archives)

transportation. Within four months, an estimated 70,000 students had participated in the rides, and approximately 3,600 were arrested. This concerted challenge to racism and segregation peaked in August 1963 with the March on Washington, D.C., which James Farmer also helped to organize.

In 1966 Farmer resigned from CORE to direct a national adult literacy project. Following a failed attempt at winning a congressional seat, President Richard M. Nixon appointed him Assistant Secretary of Health, Education and Welfare.

In 1971, Farmer left the Nixon administration to work for the Council on Minority Planning and Strategy, an African-American think tank. He also served as distinguished professor of history at Mary Washington College in Fredericksburg, Virginia, where he taught civil rights history. Dr. Farmer, the author of *Freedom When?*, completed his autobiography, *Lay Bare the Heart*, in 1985. And in 1998, less than a year before his death, he was awarded the Presidential Medal of Freedom, our nation's highest civilian award.

HOPPING JOHN DIP

In many African-American and southern homes, the New Year's Day dinner begins with the ceremonious passing of a large dish filled with "hopping john." Hopping john is a blend of black-eyed peas, ham, and rice. This traditional dish, thought to bring good luck in the coming year, is adapted here as a dip to serve while watching the bowl games.

8	slices bacon		2	cups chicken broth
1	cup onion, chopped		½	teaspoon salt
¼	cup green bell pepper, chopped		¼	cup rice, uncooked
1	teaspoon fresh jalapeño, chopped		2	teaspoons fresh lemon juice
1	garlic clove, minced		½	cup ham, finely chopped
1	10-ounce package frozen black-eyed peas			Cayenne pepper to taste

Fry bacon until crisp and remove to a paper towel–lined plate to drain. Reserve bacon drippings in pan. Add onion, green pepper, jalapeño, and garlic to pan and sauté, stirring constantly. Continue to cook until the onion is transparent. Add black-eyed peas, chicken broth, and salt. Cover and cook over medium heat for 15 minutes, stir in rice, and re-cover. Reduce heat to low and cook for 25 to 30 minutes or until the rice is cooked through. Allow mixture to cool before placing in a food processor or blender to puree. Add lemon juice. If mixture is too thick, add additional chicken broth. Garnish with chopped ham and a sprinkle of cayenne pepper and crumbled bacon. Serve with corn chips.

12 servings

BLACK BEAN DIP

Heart-healthy beans are as rich in fiber as they are in flavor. The proof is found in this delicious bean dip recipe.

1	15-ounce can black beans, drained	¼	teaspoon onion powder
½	cup mayonnaise	⅛	teaspoon cumin
½	cup sour cream	1	tablespoon olive oil
1	fresh jalapeño pepper, seeded and finely minced	1	large tomato, seeded and coarsely chopped
1	large clove garlic, minced		Salt to taste
½	teaspoon chili powder		Sour cream
			Sliced green onions

Place beans in a mixing bowl and coarsely mash. Combine mayonnaise and sour cream, mix well, and add to the bowl together with the next 6 ingredients. Mix well. Add tomato and mix until just blended. Add salt to taste and chill for 1 hour before serving. Garnish with a dollop of sour cream and a sprinkling of sliced green onions just before serving.

8 servings

In the spring of 1942, a man fresh out of theology school sat down at the counter of Chicago's Jack Spratt Coffee Shop and ordered a doughnut. Because he was black, he was refused. Because his name was James Farmer, he did not give in.

James Farmer . . . went on to help bring down Jim Crow by leading freedom rides, voter drives, and marches, enduring repeated beatings and jailings along the way. He has never sought the limelight and until today, I, frankly, think he's never gotten the credit he deserves for the contribution he has made to the freedom of African-Americans and other minorities and their equal opportunities in America. But today, he can't avoid the limelight, and his long-overdue recognition has come to pass.

—President William Jefferson Clinton, upon awarding the Presidential Medal of Freedom to James Farmer on January 15, 1998

BLACK OLIVE, JALAPEÑO, AND TOMATO MOJO

Mojo is the African-American version of salsa. I hope you enjoy this one!

3	fresh jalapeños, seeded and finely chopped	3	tablespoons olive oil
4	ounces black olives, chopped	2	tablespoons red wine vinegar
¼	cup green onion, chopped		Salt and pepper to taste
1	large clove of garlic, finely minced		Toasted Rosemary Bread (see recipe below)
3	tomatoes, seeded and finely chopped		or
		1	baguette, cut into ½-inch slices and lightly toasted

Combine first 8 ingredients, mix well, and refrigerate at least 1 hour before serving with toasted Rosemary Bread or toasted baguettes.

12 to 14 servings

ROSEMARY BREAD

Bar your guests from the kitchen while this bread is cooling or there will be none left for dipping! Day-old Rosemary Bread also makes excellent croutons. See directions for making croutons on page 120.

1½	cups warm water	3	tablespoons olive oil
2	envelopes dry yeast	1¼	tablespoons dried rosemary, crushed
1	tablespoon sugar	1½	teaspoons salt
5	cups bread flour		

In a large bowl combine the water, yeast, and sugar. Add 1¼ cups of the flour. Mix to blend and allow to stand at room temperature for 1 hour. Add the olive oil, rosemary, and salt to the yeast mixture and mix well. Add enough of the remaining flour to form a soft dough. Turn dough onto a floured surface and knead until it is smooth and elastic, approximately 8 minutes. Add more flour if the dough is sticky. However, be careful not to knead it too much or the dough will be too tough. Place dough in a large, well-oiled bowl and turn it to coat. Cover the bowl and allow dough to rise in a warm, draft-free area until doubled, approximately 1 hour.

Punch the dough down and knead until it is smooth. Divide the dough and form each half into a smooth ball. Place balls on a lightly floured baking sheet with sufficient space to allow for expansion and rising. Flatten each ball slightly to form a flat bottom on the bread. Cover each round of bread with a clean, dry tea towel. Allow bread to rise in a draft-free area until doubled in volume, approximately 1 hour.

Place bread in a preheated 400°F oven for approximately 35 to 40 minutes or until the bread is brown and the loaves sound hollow when tapped on the bottom. Set aside on racks to cool. Serve hot or toasted with mojo or flavored or plain olive oil.

Yields 2 loaves

Anna Pauli Murray

Being one of only four black women to graduate from Hunter College in 1933 was, as Anna Pauli Murray described it, her "first successful milestone." It was one of many for this civil rights advocate, feminist, lawyer, poet, teacher, and ordained minister.

Born in Baltimore, Maryland, on November 20, 1910, Murray was reared by relatives following the deaths of her parents. Her father had been a Howard University graduate who taught at a local high school. After graduating at the head of her high school class, Murray eventually earned a juris doctorate from Howard in 1944, a masters of law from the University of California, and a J.S.D. from Yale, becoming the first African-American to be awarded that degree. Her dissertation was titled, "Roots of the Racial Crisis: Prologue to Policy."

Her road to those honors was not direct. She had to temporarily interrupt her education in the 1930s, following the Wall Street crash. Unable to find work then, she rode the rails with the hobo community in search of employment. She eventually found work with the W.P.A., the Harlem Y.W.C.A., and *Opportunity* magazine. An early and committed civil rights activist, Murray confronted racism where she found it. In 1938, she applied to the all-white University of North Carolina at Chapel Hill. In 1940, she and a friend were arrested, jailed, and fined for refusing to sit in the back of a Virginia bus. They

Delta Sigma Theta sorority, Alpha chapter
The sorority was founded at Howard University on January 13, 1913. The members' first public act as a sorority? They participated in a women's suffrage march in Washington, D.C., of course! Founding member Osceola Macarthy Adams was one of the first black actresses on Broadway and directed the theatrical debuts of Harry Belafonte and Sidney Poitier. *(Photograph courtesy Howard University Archives)*

became the earliest practitioners of the "jail-no bail" strategy, which called for refusing bail upon being jailed for protesting and was widely used in the civil rights campaigns of the 50s and 60s. This tactic called attention to the cause and reversed some of the cost of protest by placing the financial burden of jail space and food on the "jailors."

Murray entered Howard University in 1941 to become a civil rights attorney. While a student there, she joined the sit-ins that were crucial to desegregating Washington restaurants and other public facilities. She later wrote that she learned at Howard "to wage an effective struggle against Jim Crow." In 1942, Murray, together with George Houser, James Farmer, and Bayard Rustin, formed the Congress of Racial Equality (CORE).

After graduating from Howard University in 1944, Murray attended the University of California, where the subject of her master's thesis was *the right to equal opportunity in employment.*

In 1960 President John F. Kennedy appointed Murray to his Committee on Civil and Political Rights. In the decade that followed, Murray eagerly embraced the burgeoning feminist movement, becoming a co-founder of the National Organization for Women. She co-wrote position papers on the E.R.A. and Title VII of the 1964 Civil Rights Act and the American Civil Liberties Union brief for *White v. Crook,* a case that successfully challenged all-white, all-male juries. In 1977 Murray became the first African-American woman ordained as an Episcopal priest and performed her first Holy Eucharist in the same North Carolina chapel where her grandmother, a slave, had been baptized.

VEGETABLE DIP

1	cup sour cream	1	teaspoon cilantro, minced
1	cup mayonnaise	1	cup parsley, finely minced
1	teaspoon garlic salt	⅛	teaspoon Tabasco sauce
1½	tablespoons dill weed, minced	1	tablespoon olive oil
			Paprika

Combine the above ingredients, mix well, and refrigerate at least an hour. Garnish with paprika before serving with vegetable crudités and assorted crackers.

8 to 16 servings

CLAM DIP

¼ cup green bell peppers, chopped	1 tablespoon Worcestershire sauce
1 cup celery, chopped	1 (8-ounce) package cream cheese, softened
¼ cup green onions, including tops, sliced	2 cans minced clams
3 tablespoons fresh lemon juice	1 cup mayonnaise

Combine above ingredients, mix well, and refrigerate for an hour before serving. Serve with vegetable crudités or chips.

Yields approximately 2½ cups

HOT CRABMEAT BREAD BOWL

This tasty, hot, crabmeat bread bowl presents beautifully and promises to be the belle of the ball!

1 large round of crusty bread	1 teaspoon lemon juice
2 cans crabmeat	2 teaspoons Worcestershire sauce
1 16-ounce package cream cheese, softened	¼ cup onion, finely chopped
¼ cup sour cream	½ teaspoon paprika
	Cayenne pepper to taste

Preheat oven to 275°F. Cut off top ⅓ of bread and set aside for later use as a "bowl lid." Hollow the bottom ⅓ of bread to form the "bowl" and set aside. Cut bread removed from the bowl into cubes and set aside. In a separate bowl, combine remaining ingredients and mix well. Pour the mixture into the hollowed bread, cover with bread lid, and wrap in aluminum foil; bake in the preheated oven for an hour. Remove foil and serve with toasted bread cubes and baguette slices.

8 to 10 servings

CRABMEAT-STUFFED MUSHROOMS

8	ounces fresh mushrooms, stems removed		1	teaspoon parsley, finely minced
2	8-ounce packages cream cheese, softened		½	pound cooked crabmeat
2	tablespoons green onion, finely chopped		1	tablespoon sherry
2	tablespoons pecans, finely chopped		1	dash garlic powder
				Salt and pepper to taste
				Paprika for garnish

Wipe mushroom caps clean and refrigerate. Combine remaining ingredients, mix well, and refrigerate for approximately 1 hour. Spoon mixture into mushroom caps and garnish with paprika immediately prior to serving.

Yields approximately 25 stuffed mushroom caps

SAUSAGE-STUFFED MUSHROOM CAPS

These yummy mushroom caps disappear quickly, so make extras!

24	large mushroom caps		½	teaspoon dried thyme
8	ounces ground sausage meat		¼	teaspoon dried tarragon
½	small onion, finely chopped			Salt and pepper to taste
1	garlic clove, finely minced		4	tablespoons olive oil, divided
2	tablespoons fresh parsley, chopped, divided		½	cup fresh bread crumbs

Preheat oven to 375°F. Wipe the mushrooms clean, cut away and discard any dirty or woody stem ends, and remove the stems carefully. Avoid damaging the caps.

Finely chop stems and combine with the sausage meat, onion, garlic, half the parsley, thyme, and tarragon. Mix well and season to taste with salt and freshly ground black pepper.

Pour 1 tablespoon olive oil in a heavy pan and heat it over a moderate burner or flame. Add the sausage meat mixture and cook for about 5 minutes, crumbling and blending it with a fork until it is lightly browned. Add additional olive oil as needed. Remove the pan from the heat and allow the mixture to cool.

Evenly divide the mixture and stuff the caps. Combine bread crumbs and remaining parsley. Sprinkle over the stuffed mushrooms and bake in the preheated oven for 20 minutes or until the tops are nicely browned. Serve immediately.

Yields 24 stuffed mushroom caps

The Congress on Racial Equality (CORE)

CORE is the third oldest and one of the "Big Four" civil rights groups in the United States. From the protests against "Jim Crow" laws of the 40s to the "Sit-ins" of the 50s and the "Freedom Rides" of the 60s; through the cries for "Self-Determination" in the 70s and "Equal Opportunity" in the 80s to the struggle for community development in the 90s, CORE has championed true equality for all people. As the "shock troops" and pioneers of the civil rights movement, CORE has paved the way for the nation to follow. As we approach the end of the 20th century, CORE has turned its focus to preparing minorities for the technical and skills demands of the new millennium.

—www.core-online.org/features/what_is_core

Founded in 1942 by Howard University graduates James Farmer and Anna Pauli Murray, among others CORE is a Chicago-based civil rights organization dedicated to nonviolent social activism. Seeking to enhance race relations and end racial discrimination in Chicago, the organization initially directed its attention to desegregating public accommodations in that city. Later its program of nonviolent sit-ins was expanded to the South, where CORE gained national recognition by sponsoring the 1961 Freedom Rides. CORE was a sponsor of the 1963 civil rights March on Washington. After the resignation of director James Farmer in 1966 it changed its focus to black voter registration in the South and community issues.

ANGELS IN BLANKETS

48 large shrimp	½ teaspoon Worcestershire sauce
½ cup Dijon-style mustard	24 slices Canadian bacon, cut in half

Shell, devein, and wash shrimp under cold running water; pat dry and set aside. Combine mustard and Worcestershire sauce, mix well, and brush each slice of bacon with this mixture. Wrap each shrimp with a bacon slice and secure with a toothpick. Place shrimp in broiler, approximately 6 inches from heat source, and broil 3 to 4 minutes. Turn shrimp and broil an additional 2 to 3 minutes.

Yields 48 hors d'oeuvres

GRILLED CHILI SHRIMP

¼ cup fresh grapefruit juice	½ teaspoon ground pepper
2 teaspoons fresh lime juice	Pinch of cayenne pepper
1¾ teaspoons chili powder	1 pound large shrimp, peeled and deveined
⅛ teaspoon cumin	
⅓ teaspoon garlic powder	¼ cup (½ stick) melted butter
¼ teaspoon onion powder	

Combine first 8 ingredients and add shrimp; refrigerate and marinate for 1 hour, turning once. Thread shrimp on bamboo or metal skewers and brush with butter. Grill over a medium fire for 2 to 3 minutes on each side or until shrimp are opaque and their tails slightly curled.

4 servings

EAST COAST CRAB CAKES

1	pound processed crabmeat	1	teaspoon seafood seasoning
1	egg, beaten		Cream Sauce *(see below)*
3	tablespoons mayonnaise	2	eggs, beaten
1	teaspoon dry mustard		Bread crumbs
½	teaspoon salt		Shortening
	Dash of hot pepper sauce (optional)		

Pick over crabmeat to remove any foreign objects and set aside. Combine next 6 ingredients and mix with crabmeat; blend well. Add cream sauce to mixture (see recipe below). Form into 6 to 8 crab cakes. Dip crab cakes into egg and bread crumbs; repeat procedure and place crab cakes on a wax paper–lined cookie sheet and chill 1 hour before frying. Fry in ⅔ inches of shortening over medium-high heat until cakes are golden. Do not crowd pan.

6 to 8 servings

CREAM SAUCE

1	tablespoon melted butter	2	tablespoons half-and-half
1½	teaspoons flour		

Combine the above ingredients and mix well to blend.

Freedom Rides

At our first stop in Virginia . . . I [was] confronted with what the Southern white has called "separate but equal." A modern rest station with gleaming counters and picture windows was labeled "White," and a small wooden shack beside it was tagged "Colored."

—Freedom Rider William Mahoney

Hard-fought battles won in the courtroom were often not enforced in the community, especially in the South. As early as 1947, CORE planned a "journey of reconciliation" in which they planned to test the decision reached in *Morgan v. Virginia,* which had declared the segregated seating of interstate passengers to be unconstitutional.

"This was not civil disobedience, really," explained CORE director James Farmer, "because we [were] merely doing what the Supreme Court said we had a right to do." But the Freedom Riders expected to meet resistance. "We felt we could count on the racists of the South to create a crisis so that the federal government would be compelled to enforce the law," said Farmer. Their efforts were met with violent resistance, with some members of the group being arrested and forced to serve time on a chain gang. However, according to Farmer, "When we began the ride I think all of us were prepared for as much violence as could be thrown at us. We were prepared for the possibility of death."

The journey of reconciliation was abandoned and would not be attempted again until a decade and a half later, when once again, the strategy called for an interracial group to board buses destined for the South, with whites sitting in the back and blacks in the front. The Freedom Ride that left Washington, D.C., on May 4, 1961, was scheduled to arrive in New Orleans on May 17, the seventh anniversary of the *Brown v. Board of Education Topeka* decision.

On Mother's Day, May 14, the Freedom Riders split into two groups. An angry mob of approximately 200 people met the first group in Anniston, Alabama. Although the bus was stoned and its tires slashed, the riders managed to escape. However, when they stopped six miles outside of town to change the tires, the bus was firebombed. The other group did not fare any better. In Birmingham, the second group was also received by a mob and riders were severely beaten. Despite the violence and threats to their lives, the Freedom

Riders, most notable among them Jim Peck, a white rider who received fifty stitches for his injuries, were determined to continue. Peck insisted, "I think it is particularly important at this time when it has become national news that we continue and show that non-violence can prevail over violence."

When this first ride ended the bus company refused to risk losing another bus or drivers. Despite the beatings and arrests, despite the denial of their civil rights in courts (on one occasion, a judge turned his back on the defendants as their attorney presented their defense and only turned to face them when he handed down a sentence of sixty days in the state penitentiary) more Freedom Riders continued to arrive. By summer's end, more than 300 had been arrested. Although none reached New Orleans, and many spent their summer in jail while others were scarred for life by the beatings they received, their efforts were not in vain. As a result of the adverse publicity, the Kennedy administration was forced to take action: At the request of Robert Kennedy, the Interstate Commerce Commission (ICC) outlawed segregation in interstate bus travel.

TEACUP CRAB CHOWDER

I enjoy serving this chowder as an appetizer because it is quick, elegant, and keeps my guests satisfied while I finalize the meal.

1 tablespoon butter	1 pint whipping cream
3 tablespoons sliced green onions	1 cup half-and-half
1⅓ cups (8 ounces) pasteurized crabmeat	⅛ teaspoon nutmeg
	Nutmeg to garnish

In a saucepan sauté onions in butter for 1 minute; add crabmeat and mix well. Add next three ingredients, mix to blend and heat through. Garnish with a dash of nutmeg before serving in warmed teacups with teaspoons.

4 servings

HEAVENLY STUFFED EGG HALVES

Why should the devil receive credit for this heavenly appetizer?

12	hard-boiled eggs, halved lengthwise		¼	teaspoon salt
⅓	cup mayonnaise		¼	teaspoon cayenne pepper
1	teaspoon Dijon-style mustard		⅛	teaspoon cumin
¼	teaspoon prepared horseradish		½	cup cooked crabmeat
1¼	tablespoons shallots, finely chopped			Ground paprika

Remove egg yolks from the egg halves and reserve whites. Place yolks in a bowl, mash, combine with remaining ingredients, and mix well. Add additional mayonnaise as necessary to reach the desired consistency. Mixture should hold its own shape without being too runny. Spoon or pipe into reserved egg whites and refrigerate, covered lightly with plastic wrap for at least 1 hour. Garnish with paprika before serving.

24 servings

EGGPLANT AND TOMATO DIP

1	large eggplant		⅓	cup fresh lemon juice
2	medium tomatoes, diced		½	teaspoon salt
¼	cup onion, finely chopped		3	cloves minced garlic
3	tablespoons parsley, chopped			Toasted sesame seeds for garnish
½	cup olive oil			

Preheat oven to 350°F. Wash the eggplant and pierce it several times with a fork before placing it in the oven to bake for 45 minutes. Remove from oven and immediately dip the eggplant in cold water, then peel. Chop eggplant flesh and place in a serving bowl. Add remaining ingredients and marinate in the refrigerator overnight. This dip will keep for several days in the refrigerator. Garnish with toasted sesame seeds immediately before serving it with pita triangles for dipping.

12 servings

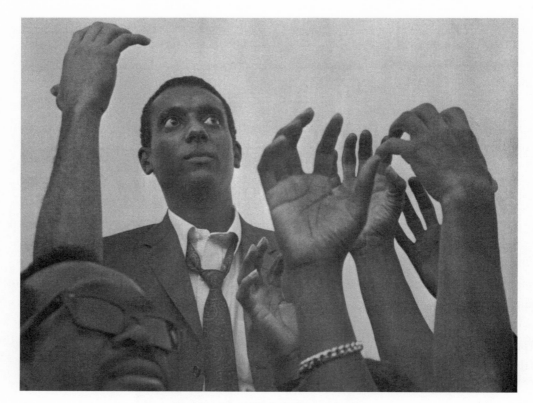

Kwame Ture (Stokely Carmichael),
legendary student civil rights activist
(Corbis)

Kwame Ture (Stokely Carmichael)

My name is Mabel Carmichael. Two generations of Movement youth know me
as May Charles. Kwame Ture (also known as Stokely Carmichael) is my son.
Fifty-eight years ago, I brought Kwame into this world. Thirty-nine years ago,
I gave him to the people, to the Movement, to the Nonviolent Action Group
at Howard University, and the Student Non-Violent Coordinating Committee,
its parent organization.

—Mrs. Mabel Carmichael, December 4, 1999

Kwame Ture, born Stokely Carmichael to working-class parents in Port of Spain, Trinidad, rose through the ranks of Howard's Non-Violent Action Group and the National Student Non-Violent Coordinating Committee to become a powerfully eloquent and radical voice for the civil and human rights movements.

Following his move to the United States, Carmichael attended the prestigious Bronx High School of Science. In 1960 he entered Howard University, where he studied philosophy.

During the 60s, students around the country were organizing groups such as NAG (the Non-Violent Action Group) at Howard University. Carmichael, a founding member of NAG, was also active in the Congress of Racial Equality. Later he joined the Student Non-Violent Coordinating Committee (SNCC) and was elected its national chairman in June 1966. He courageously participated in Freedom Rides, sit-ins, voter registration drives, and other demonstrations to challenge discrimination in the segregated South.

While in Greenwood, Mississippi, Carmichael and friend Willie Ricks introduced the phrase "Black Power," which became a rallying cry of the civil rights movement. In 1966 he left SNCC and briefly joined the Black Panthers as the prime minister of the party, headquartered in Oakland, California. When he became disenchanted with the Panthers, he moved to Guinea, West Africa.

While in Africa, Stokely Carmichael became Kwame Ture to honor Kwame Nkrumah, who led Ghana to independence from Britain; and Ahmed Sekou Toure, the president of Guinea, who was his friend and mentor. He led the All-African People's Revolutionary Party for more than thirty years and devoted himself to Pan Africanism. To the end of his life he answered his telephone by announcing, *"Ready for the revolution."*

HOT CHICKEN, FETA, AND ARTICHOKE DIP

This hearty, hot dip is sure to delight your guests!

2	cups cooked chicken breast, coarsely chopped	1	cup plus 1 tablespoon mayonnaise
1	14-ounce can artichoke hearts, drained and coarsely chopped	½	cup grated Parmesan cheese
		1	2-ounce jar diced pimentos, drained
		¼	cup ripe olives, drained and chopped
2	4-ounce packages feta cheese, crumbled	1	clove garlic, minced
			Dash of cayenne pepper

Preheat oven to 350°F. Combine all the ingredients and mix well. Spoon mixture into a 3-cup, shallow baking dish; bake for 20 to 25 minutes or until lightly browned. Serve with pita triangles or assorted crackers.

Yields 2 cups

HOT AND SPICY PARTY MEATBALLS

3	pounds 98% lean ground beef	3	cloves garlic, minced
6	eggs, well beaten	4½	tablespoons horseradish
1½	cups dry bread crumbs	7	drops Tabasco sauce
		2¼	teaspoons seasoned salt

Preheat the oven to 375°F. Combine all the ingredients and mix well; shape into 100 bite-size meatballs. Place the meatballs on two baking sheets and bake for 15 minutes or until browned. When the meatballs are done remove them to a paper towel–lined plate to drain. Serve with Spicy Meatball Sauce (recipe follows).

Yields 100 meatballs

SPICY MEATBALL SAUCE

2   cups tomato catsup
1   cup chili sauce
2   cups water
1   cup cider vinegar
2   tablespoons grape jelly

1¼ cup minced onions
½   cup Worcestershire sauce
1½ teaspoons salt
¼   teaspoon Tabasco sauce
    Pinch of cayenne pepper

Combine all the ingredients in a large saucepan, mix well, and bring to a quick boil. Reduce heat and simmer 15 minutes. Place meatballs in sauce, mix gently, and allow them to warm through before serving with toothpicks.

Yields 6 cups

HOT STEAK BITES

4   boneless rib eye steaks, cut
    1 inch thick
    (approximately 2½ pounds)
½   cup jalapeño jelly
3   tablespoons steak seasonings

¼   cup fresh jalapeño peppers, seeded
    and finely chopped
    Red bell pepper strips, (½-inch
    wide) grilled, sautéed, or broiled

Wash the steaks under cold running water, pat dry, season to taste, and set aside. Combine the next 3 ingredients in a small saucepan and cook over medium heat until jelly dissolves. Remove from heat and set aside. Steaks may be broiled or grilled. If you elect to broil the steaks, place them on the unheated rack of a broiler pan 3 to 4 inches from the heat and broil to the desired degree of doneness. Allow 12 to 15 minutes' cooking time for medium-rare steaks (center of meat is 145°) or 15 to 18 minutes for medium steaks (center of meat is 160°). To grill the steaks, place them on the heated rack over medium-hot coals. Grill to desired doneness, turning once during the cooking process. Brush steaks with jalapeño glaze during the last 5 minutes of cooking time. Sprinkle one or two steaks with minced jalapeño, leaving the others plain for less adventuresome palates. Cut steaks into 1-inch cubes, wrap a pepper strip around each cube, and secure with a toothpick.

Yields approximately 48 appetizers

Vernon Jordan

You are where you are today because you stand on somebody's shoulders.
And wherever you are heading, you cannot get there by yourself.

If you stand on the shoulders of others, you have a reciprocal responsibility to live
your life so that others may stand on your shoulders. It's the quid pro quo of life.

We exist temporarily through what we take, but we live forever through
what we give.

—Vernon E. Jordan, Jr., senior managing director
of Lazard Frères & Co. LLC, New York (Howard University School of Law class of 1960)

In providing strong shoulders on which the next generation could stand, Vernon Jordan's contributions to the civil rights movement alone were overwhelming and included the following: president and chief executive officer of the National Urban League; executive director of the United Negro College Fund; director of the Voter Education Project of the Southern Regional Council; attorney-consultant, U.S. Office of Economic Opportunity; assistant to the executive director of the Southern Regional Council; Georgia field director of the National Association for the Advancement of Colored People; and an attorney in private practice in Arkansas and Georgia.

Winning legal team
Thurgood Marshall *(center)* with George E. C. Hayes *(left)* and James Nabrit, Jr. *(right)*, following
their victory in *Brown v. Board of Education.*
(Corbis)

The Long Walk to Equality:
Significant Moments in the Civil Rights Movement

1941

Franklin D. Roosevelt signs an executive order banning discrimination in employment by government defense contractors.

1942

Founding of the Congress of Racial Equality (CORE).

1946

President Harry S. Truman addresses the national problem of racial discrimination by establishing the President's Committee on Civil Rights.

U.S. Supreme Court bans segregation in interstate bus travel.

1947

The first Freedom Riders, led by CORE, travel through the South to test the Supreme Court decision banning segregation in interstate bus travel.

Baseball's color barrier is broken by Jackie Robinson when he is signed by the Brooklyn Dodgers, becoming the first black to play major league sports in half a century.

1948

Supreme Court rules that federal and state courts cannot enforce laws that bar persons from owning property based on race. President Truman orders the integration of all units of the U.S. armed forces.

1949

CORE stages a sit-in demonstration against segregated facilities in St. Louis, Missouri.

1954

Brown v. Board of Education is decided by the the U.S. Supreme Court, overturning the "separate but equal" doctrine by finding separate educational facilities to be inherently unequal and ordering the admission of blacks to public schools on a racially nondiscriminatory basis. Nine of the ten attorneys arguing the case are Howard graduates or faculty members.

1955

Montgomery Boycott, led by Dr. Martin Luther King, Jr., successfully integrates the city's public bus system and sets precedent for other Southern cities.

1957

President Dwight D. Eisenhower protects black civil rights by using federal troops to enforce the right of nine black students to enroll at Central High School in Little Rock, Arkansas.

The Southern Christian Leadership Conference (SCLC) is established with Martin Luther King, Jr., as its first president.

The U.S. Commission on Civil Rights and a civil division in the Department of Justice is created by the United States Congress.

1960

Black students from North Carolina Agricultural and Technical College begin sit-ins in the segregated public restaurants and lunch counters of Greensboro, North Carolina.

Student Nonviolent Coordinating Committee (SNCC) is founded at Shaw University in Raleigh, North Carolina.

1961

Freedom Riders begin their campaign to desegregate drinking fountains, lunch counters, rest rooms, and waiting rooms in bus and train stations in the South by deliberately violating "white only" rules at those locations.

The Committee on Equal Employment Opportunity is established by President John F. Kennedy.

Thurgood Marshall is appointed to the U.S. Circuit Court of Appeals.

The University of Georgia admits black students in accordance with federal court orders.

1962
Voter registration drives begin in Mississippi with students like Howard's Stokely
Carmichael at the forefront.

James Meredith, a black student, requires the protection of federal troops to enroll at
the University of Mississippi.

President Kennedy orders the end of discriminatory practices in federally funded public
housing.

1963
"Birmingham Sunday": Segregationists bomb a Baptist church, killing four black
children.

Attended by 250,000 people nationwide, the March on Washington culminates in
Dr. Martin Luther King, Jr.'s, famous "I Have a Dream" speech.

Federal troops are dispatched by President John F. Kennedy to enforce the enrollment
rights of black students at the University of Alabama.

Medgar Evers, a field secretary for the National Association for the Advancement of
Colored People (NAACP), is assassinated in Jackson, Mississippi.

1965
Voting Rights Act permitting federal examiners to register black voters in certain
circumstances is enacted, resulting in the registration of more than half of eligible
blacks in Alabama, Mississippi, Louisiana, Georgia, and South Carolina, and the
election of more blacks than ever to public office.

President Lyndon Johnson declares "War on Poverty" by initiating public programs
directed at providing job training, housing, education, health care, and other social
benefits for the poor.

1966
Stokely Carmichael becomes national president of SNCC.

1967
Thurgood Marshall is the first black appointed to the United States Supreme Court.

1968

Plans are announced by Dr. Martin Luther King, Jr., for the Poor People's Campaign in Washington, D.C.; among the demands are employment for all Americans.

Dr. Martin Luther King, Jr. is assassinated in Memphis. Ralph Abernathy is named head of SCLC, and Andrew Young becomes its vice-president.

Discrimination in the rental and sale of all housing is prohibited by the U.S. Supreme Court.

1970

The Office of Minority Business Enterprise is created by President Richard M. Nixon to help minorities succeed in business.

1971

The United States Supreme Court upholds school busing as a means of achieving desegregation.

1972

Equal Opportunity and Employment Act is passed.

1978

The United States Supreme Court decides Bakke, which legalizes the concept of "reverse" discrimination. Amicus brief filed by Howard Professor Herbert Odré Reid, Sr.

1982

The Voting Rights Act is strengthened and extended for twenty-five years.

1983

President Ronald Reagan signs legislation designating Martin Luther King, Jr.'s birthday a national holiday.

1989

Howard graduate L. Douglas Wilder is elected governor of Virginia, becoming the first black to be elected governor of a state.

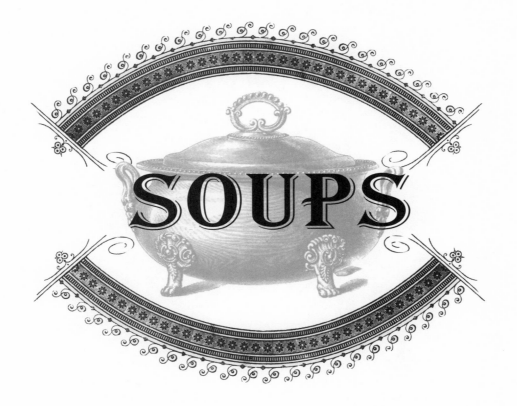

SOUPS

Ralph Bunche
A Howard University professor and UN ambassador, Bunche was the first
African-American to receive the Nobel Peace Prize.
(Corbis)

Political, International, and National Affairs

Our department of political science owes much to Dr. Bunche, who helped organize it in 1928. Because of Bunche and others who followed in the footsteps of this formidable African-American scholar and statesman, Howard has become an outward-looking institution fully engaged in national security issues and in a wide variety of international programs spanning the globe.

—H. Patrick Swygert, president of Howard University,
The Philadelphia Inquirer, July 11, 1998

Men and women are usually products of their times, but only a few can be said to have influenced their times. Bunche was such a person. The little more than five decades between Bunche's student days and his death were marked by many momentous developments in the world, none more telling than the . . . resolute movement of "people of color" in the United States and throughout the world, for freedom and equality . . . and the establishment of new world institutions dedicated to the achievement of peace and justice among all peoples.

—Dr. Benjamin Rivlin, co-chair of the Ralph Bunche
Centenary Commemoration Committee and director emeritus
of the Ralph Bunche Institute for International Studies

Howard University Professor Ralph Johnson Bunche, scholar, civil rights activist, U.S. diplomat, statesman, and United Nations Under-Secretary-General, was the son of Fred Bunch, a barber, and Olive Agnes Johnson Bunch, an amateur musician. Born on

August 7, 1903, he would overcome personal tragedy and racial barriers to greatly influ-ence the course of world events and become the first person of color to receive the Nobel Peace Prize, awarded in 1950. At first he declined the award, which recognized his suc-cessful negotiation of an Arab-Israeli truce in Palestine, stating that he was in the UN Sec-retariat and only doing his job, for which he could not receive a prize. The armistice was the United Nations' first concrete success in containing war in the Middle East. Later, after being contacted by the committee, the secretary-general, Trygve Lie, prevailed upon Bunche to accept the prize "for the good of the United Nations. . . ."

In receiving the Nobel Prize, this peacemaker was selected over Winston Churchill and George C. Marshall, icons of World War II. Receipt of this highly coveted award was the highlight of a distinguished career, which encompassed cutting-edge civil rights and racial equality work in the United States; development of a greater understanding of Africa; establishment of the United Nations, the noteworthy development of innovative programs for international mediation, and the containment of armed conflict through international peacekeeping operations.

Throughout his life, Bunche would attribute his success to his maternal grandmother, Mrs. Lucy Taylor Johnson, or "Nana," who lived with the family. When he was ten years old the family moved to Albuquerque, New Mexico, for reasons related to his parents' health. Tragically, both parents died two years later, after which Nana moved Ralph and his two sisters to Los Angeles. (It was at this time that she added the "e" to the spelling of their surname.) He graduated with honors from the Los Angeles 30th Street Interme-diate School. Had it not been for the intervention of his indomitable grandmother, Bunche would have continued in the "practical" or industrial courses to which he'd been assigned because of his race. At her insistence, he was placed in academic courses to prepare him for college.

In 1922, he broke a race barrier by graduating first in his class and as valedictorian from Jefferson High School. However, despite his extraordinary academic achievement, he was denied election to the city-wide scholarship honor society. Of his experiences Bunche would later write, "I wasn't embittered . . . for Nana had taught me to fight with-out rancor. She taught all of us to stand up for our rights, to suffer no indignity, but to harbor no bitterness toward anyone. . . . Deeply religious, she instilled in us a sense of personal pride . . . but she also taught us understanding and tolerance."

Following high school graduation, Bunche was admitted to the southern branch of the University of California on an academic scholarship. Once again, he thrived in the competitive academic environment, excelling in philosophy and political science and eventually becoming a member of Phi Beta Kappa. He shone outside of the classroom as well: He wrote for the school newspaper, won oratorical contests as president of the debating society, was sports editor of the yearbook, and a student council leader, and a standout in varsity basketball, playing guard for three years on championship teams.

In 1927, after graduating summa cum laude with a degree in international relations and serving as class valedictorian, he entered Harvard University, which awarded him a scholarship to study political science. After completing his M.A. in 1928 and while completing his doctoral studies as an Ozias Goodwin Fellow at Harvard, Bunche joined the faculty of Howard University, where for a time he served as assistant to Mordecai Johnson, the school's first black president. He also organized and chaired Howard's first political science department and organized the Joint Committee on National Recovery to lobby Congress for black participation in New Deal programs and to fight against racial discrimination in New Deal agencies. It was also at Howard that Mortimer Weaver, a former Howard teacher, introduced Bunche to his future wife, Ruth Ethel Harris, a first-grade teacher in Washington.

Over the next six years, Bunche alternated between teaching and working toward his doctorate. In 1934 he became the first black man to receive a Ph.D. in government and international relations at Harvard and was awarded the coveted Toppan Prize for the year's best dissertation in political science.

I have a deep-seated bias against hate and intolerance. I have a bias against racial and religious bigotry. I have a bias against war; a bias for peace. I have a bias that leads me to believe in the essential goodness of my fellow man; which leads me to believe that no problem of human relations is ever insoluble.

—Dr. Ralph Bunche

During the 1930s, Howard University continued to attract young, black scholar-activists, concerned with the unequal treatment of African-Americans. Howard was an intellectual Mecca for these students, and Dr. Bunche, often viewed as a radical teacher, was their leader. In addition to providing intellectual leadership, Dr. Bunche offered his home on the Howard campus as a meeting and gathering place. In the words of Dr. Charles Henry, Dr. Bunche was the "true model of a scholar-activist."

We can never have too much preparation and training. We must be a strong competitor. We must adhere staunchly to the basic principle that anything less than full equality is not enough. . . .

—Dr. Ralph Bunche

In particular, Bunche was active in the struggle for civil rights and racial equality. In 1935, he was instrumental in organizing a conference at Howard University, which assessed the New Deal's economic impact on African-Americans. In 1936, he was a founder of the National Negro Congress, which unified Negro leaders. During that same year, he launched a successful protest against the presentation of *Porgy and Bess* at Washington's segregated National Theater. The theater was desegregated during the run of the play.

Important as Dr. Bunche's work in the United Nations has been, I remember him best for his early commitment to the civil rights campaigns during the 1930s and 1940s. Our movement was young then, and it was totally committed young people like Ralph Bunche, whose spirit and resilience, in the face of overwhelming odds, gave strength to the rest of us.

—A. Philip Randolph, labor activist and civil rights pioneer

The advent of World War II shifted Bunche's focus to the international arena. Following U.S. entry into the war, Dr. Bunche took a leave of absence from Howard to accept a position with the Office of the Coordinator of Information, where he served as a specialist on colonialism and race relations. When the department was redesigned as the Office of Strategic Services, he was elevated to head the Africa Section in the Research and Analysis Branch. In 1944, Dr. Bunche transferred to the State Department's postwar planning group, where he began working on the issue of the future of the colonial world. He advised members of the American delegation at Dumbarton Oaks (1944) and the San Francisco Conference (1945), which drafted the United Nations Charter. Bunche was a key participant in drafting Chapters XI, XII, and XIII of the UN Charter, which deal with the UN policy on colonial territories.

Ralph Bunche was an international institution in his own right, transcending both nationality and race in a way that is achieved by very few.

—U Thant, Secretary-General of the United Nations, under whom Bunche served

In the fall of 1945, Bunche was a member of the preparatory commission that implemented United Nations operations. In January of 1946 he was part of the American delegation to the first session of the General Assembly. Shortly thereafter, he was selected to join the Secretariat as head of the Trusteeship Department and became department director a year later.

In 1946, the future of Palestine was a leading world issue and the item uppermost on the United Nation's agenda. Bunche's work on the United Nations Committee on Palestine (UNSCOP), which made recommendations on the division of the territory, earned him the respect of his peers at the UN, who viewed him as a keen analyst of the issues.

"Who dares to fire on peacemakers?"

—Dr. Ralph Bunche

When war erupted between the newly created state of Israel and neighboring Arab states in May 1948, Bunche was designated by Secretary-General Trygve Lie as his representative in Palestine and head of the Secretariat support staff of the UN mediator, Count Folke Bernadotte of Sweden. Upon Bernadotte's assassination in Jerusalem, Bunche was appointed acting mediator. While touring a Palestinian sector, his driver was killed by a sniper's bullet. Bunche brought the speeding vehicle to a halt before leaping from it with a UN flag in hand while bravely calling out, "Who dares to fire on peacemakers." According to reports, the guns were almost immediately silenced.

Through his perseverance and great diplomatic skill, Bunche negotiated individual armistice agreements between Israel and four Arab states, Egypt, Jordan, Syria and Lebanon. This success brought Bunche worldwide acclaim, culminating in the Nobel Peace Prize. In the United States he was widely hailed as the personification of the American dream by being the first black to receive world recognition for his extraordinary achievement. In 1949, he was awarded the Spingarn Medal by the National Association for the Advancement of Colored Peoples. (He was a director of the NAACP until his death.) The same year he received an honorary Doctor of Laws from Harvard University, one of sixty-nine honorary degrees he received. Numerous elementary and high schools throughout the country are named after Ralph Bunche, as is a park opposite United Nations headquarters in New York.

Poor health forced Bunche's retirement from the United Nations in October of 1971, and he died that year on December 9. Dr. Bunche's meteoric rise from humble beginnings to become one of the most admired human rights activists in the world continues to light the way for the rest of us.

HOPPING JOHN SOUP

Soup is a wonderful comfort food. By its very nature it invites a communal response as people gather first to enjoy the warmth of its heady aroma and stay to experience its special blends of flavor and texture.

4	strips bacon		1	tablespoon hot pepper sauce
1	large onion, finely chopped		1	teaspoon dried thyme
2	cloves garlic, minced		2	bay leaves
2	15-ounce cans of black-eyed peas, undrained		4	spicy Italian sausage links, cooked and sliced ½-inch thick
½	cup water			Salt and pepper to taste
1	14½-ounce can chicken broth		2	cups cooked rice
1	cup stewed tomatoes		2	tablespoons fresh parsley, minced
2	tablespoons molasses			

In a large pot, sauté bacon until transparent, add onions and garlic; continue to sauté until onions are tender and transparent. Add peas and their liquid, water, chicken broth, tomatoes, molasses, hot pepper sauce, thyme, and bay leaves and bring mixture to a boil. Reduce heat to low, cover, and cook for 15 minutes, stirring occasionally to prevent scorching. Add sausage during last 5 minutes of cooking time. Remove and discard bacon, add salt and pepper to taste, and keep soup warm while preparing the rice.

Combine rice and parsley, pack mixture into small ramekin bowls and unmold in soup bowls. Ladle soup around rice.

6 servings

SOUL IN A BOWL SOUP

Everything you liked best about Sunday dinner at your grandmother's house can be found in a bowl of this soup—everything except a complimentary Buttermilk Corn Muffin. For that, see the recipe on page 221.

2	large smoked ham hocks	3	tablespoons bacon drippings
3	14½-ounce cans chicken broth	3	medium onions, chopped
2	pounds fresh collard greens	1	clove garlic, minced
2	cups water	2	sweet potatoes, peeled and sliced
1	2-pound ham steak, cubed	4	16-ounce cans field peas, drained
2	tablespoons Tabasco	1	tablespoon white vinegar
		1	teaspoon salt

In a large pot combine the ham hocks with the broth and bring to a rapid boil; reduce heat to medium, cover, and simmer 1 hour. While meat is simmering, clean greens by first removing and discarding any wilted, blemished, or yellow greens. Remove and discard coarse stems and leaf midribs. Next, fill sink with cold water and wash greens by plunging them up and down in the water several times. Depending on the sandiness of your greens, you may be required to repeat this process several times. Stack 8 to 10 leaves at a time into a pile; roll them together cigar fashion and slice into ¼-inch strips. Transfer to the pot containing cooked ham hocks. Cover and simmer over medium heat for 45 minutes. Remove ham hocks from the pot. When they are sufficiently cool to handle, remove tough outer skin and bone, shred meat, and return to the pot. (For some, the outer skin is a delectable treat, so I can't in good conscience urge that it be discarded along with the bone.) Add additional broth or water as necessary to prevent scorching.

In a large skillet, toss diced ham in Tabasco and bacon drippings and sauté for 8 to 10 minutes. Add onion and garlic to the ham and sauté until onions are tender. Add ham and onion mixture to the pot of greens. Add diced potatoes, field peas, vinegar, and salt. Taste for seasoning. Simmer over low heat for 45 minutes.

8 to 10 servings

Soup Notes: **Refrain from overseasoning soup when it first begins to cook. Flavors intensify as the soup simmers. So, wait to adjust seasonings until just before serving.**

HEARTY NAVY BEAN SOUP

This soup, a favorite of my dad's, was served often in our home. In some respects the pot was almost bottomless: When it got low more water and/or cooked rice were added. There always seemed to be at least one additional bowlful available.

2 cups dried navy beans	1 bay leaf
3 tablespoons bacon drippings (may substitute vegetable oil)	½ cup carrots, grated
	2 cloves garlic
	4 tablespoons flour
1¼ cups onion, chopped	1 cup half-and-half
½ cup celery, diced	1 cup milk
½ cup green bell pepper, chopped	1½ cups ground, cooked ham
	Cayenne pepper and salt to taste
3 quarts chicken broth	Fresh minced parsley

Pick over beans to remove foreign objects, cover with water by 2 inches, and soak overnight. The next day, heat bacon drippings in a large 4½-quart pot, add onions, celery, and bell pepper, and sauté until onions are limp and tender. Add broth to the pot and bring to a boil. Drain water away from the beans, rinse them well, and add them to the pot. Bring mixture to a boil, add bay leaf, carrots, and garlic, reduce heat, and simmer gently 3 hours, or until beans are soft. Add extra boiling broth or water as needed to allow the beans to boil freely. Remove beans from heat and allow them to cool slightly, then purée the beans and set them aside, reserving the liquid. Return the cooking liquid to high heat and bring to a boil. In a small bowl, combine flour, table cream and milk, mix well; add mixture to the boiling liquid and stir to thicken. Add bean puree and ham to soup pot and simmer approximately 15 minutes. Season the soup with cayenne pepper and salt. Garnish with parsley and serve hot.

6 to 8 servings

LIMA BEAN SOUP

As a child, I had a strong dislike of lima beans. I would accept the punishment for refusing to eat them rather than eat them—that is until my mother prepared this wonderful soup. Only later did she tell me that it was lima bean soup.

2	tablespoons butter	4½	cups chicken broth
½	cup onion, finely chopped	1	medium tomato, seeded and diced
¼	cup celery, finely chopped	1½	cups half-and-half
2	cloves garlic, minced		
1	pound fresh lima beans or dried (if using dried, follow package directions as to cooking them)		

Sauté onions, celery, and garlic in butter over medium-high heat until onions are translucent. Add chicken broth and beans; bring to a boil, reduce heat and simmer 30 minutes or until the lima beans are tender. Add diced tomatoes during the last 15 minutes of cooking time. Puree half of the mixture, then return to the pot and simmer 5 additional minutes to warm through.

6 servings

SPLIT PEA SOUP

1	pound split peas	1	bay leaf
8	slices bacon		Pinch of nutmeg
2	cups onion, chopped	2	cups ham, coarsely chopped
6½	cups chicken broth		Salt and pepper to taste

Pick over peas to remove foreign objects, cover with water by 2 inches, and soak overnight. The next day, fry bacon in a heavy soup pot until crisp. Remove bacon from the pot to a paper towel–lined plate to drain. Add onions and sauté until they are transparent. Drain peas and rinse well before adding them to the pot. Stir mixture and continue to cook for 2 to 3 minutes before stirring in chicken broth and bay leaf. Cover the pot, reduce heat, and simmer for 1¼ hours. Check soup often, adding additional broth or water as needed to prevent scorching. Cook until beans are soft. Remove the lid, add nutmeg, and allow the beans to cook down until the juice reaches the desired consistency, approximately 15 minutes. If soup is too thick, thin with additional chicken broth or water. If it is not thick enough, continue to cook down. Stir in the ham and allow it to warm through. Add salt and pepper to taste. Crumble cooked bacon over individual servings to garnish.

6 servings

Howard women enjoy an organizational luncheon
(Photograph courtesy Howard University Archives)

The Ralph J. Bunche International Affairs Center

An International Affairs Center, established at Howard in 1993, was rechristened the Ralph J. Bunche International Center with United Nations Secretary-General Boutros Boutros-Ghali and the Bunche family in attendance. Today the center is the focal point of the university's many and varied international interests.

SAUSAGE AND BEAN CHOWDER

It's a chilly, rainy, mid-October afternoon and I'm thinking soup!

½ pound ground pork sausage
1 small onion, chopped
½ cup green bell pepper, chopped
1 small clove of garlic, minced
¾ teaspoon salt
¼ teaspoon thyme

1 12-ounce can tomatoes, chopped
1 15-ounce can pinto beans
2 cups chicken broth
1 bay leaf
2 teaspoons brown sugar
¾ cup potatoes, peeled and diced

Brown pork sausage in a large saucepan, while stirring and crumbling the meat. Add onion, green pepper, and garlic, continue to cook and stir another 2 to 3 minutes. Drain pan drippings and place meat mixture in a large pot. Stir in salt, thyme, chopped tomatoes, pinto beans, broth, bay leaf, and brown sugar. Bring to a quick boil, reduce heat, and simmer 1 hour. Add potatoes and cook an additional 15 minutes, or until the potatoes are fork tender.

6 servings

BLACK BEAN CHILI SOUP

2½ pounds ground chuck
1½ cups onion, diced
1   cup green pepper, diced
4   cloves garlic, crushed
4   15-ounce cans black beans
1   32-ounce can crushed
     tomatoes
2   20-ounce cans tomatoes, diced

    Juice of 3 limes
1   teaspoon Tabasco sauce
2   teaspoons cumin
1   teaspoon chili powder
¼   teaspoon garlic powder
4   cups beef broth
    Lime slices

Sauté the meat in a large pot until cooked, about 3 to 5 minutes, or until no pink remains, and then drain away the grease. Add onion and green pepper; lightly brown. Add garlic and sauté for an additional 5 to 8 minutes while stirring to blend. Add black beans, tomatoes, lime juice, Tabasco, cumin, chili powder, and garlic powder. Mix well and simmer for 30 to 35 minutes. Add beef broth 1 cup at a time to achieve the desired consistency. Serve with a slice of lime. Additional garnish suggestions: sour cream, grated Cheddar cheese, diced tomatoes, or sliced green onions.

6 to 8 servings

WHITE CHILI

1½ tablespoons vegetable oil
1½ pounds skinned, boned
     chicken breast halves,
     coarsely chopped
¾   cup leeks (white part only),
     chopped
3   garlic cloves, minced
1   14½-ounce can no-salt-added
     diced tomatoes, undrained

1   14¼-ounce can fat-free chicken
     broth
½   teaspoon dried oregano
½   teaspoon coriander seeds, crushed
¼   teaspoon ground cumin
2   16-ounce cans navy beans, drained
3   tablespoons fresh lime juice
¼   teaspoon pepper
    Shredded sharp Cheddar cheese

Sauté chicken in oil over medium-high heat for 3 minutes or until it is no longer pink. Remove chicken from pan and set aside. Add leeks and garlic to the pan and sauté 2 minutes or until the leeks are translucent. Add tomatoes and next 4 ingredients; mix to blend and bring to boil. Reduce heat and simmer 20 minutes. Add chicken and beans; cook an additional 5 minutes or until the chili is heated through. Stir in lime juice and pepper. Serve with shredded cheese.

8 servings

Slow-Cooked Black-Eyed Pea and Sweet Potato Soup

8½ cups chicken broth, approximately 5 cans	2 10-ounce packages frozen black-eyed peas, thawed
5 cloves garlic, crushed	1½ cups onion, chopped
1¼ teaspoons dried thyme	1 cup celery, diced
1 teaspoon Tabasco sauce	1 pound sweet potatoes, peeled and diced
2 bay leaves	1 red bell pepper, diced
2 smoked ham hocks	
1 pound fresh collard greens, cleaned	

Bring broth, garlic, thyme, hot sauce, and bay leaves to a boil. In the order listed, layer the remaining ingredients in a 5- to 6-quart slow cooker. Add hot broth, cover the cooker, and simmer on low for 8 to 10 hours or on high for 4 to 5 hours, until the beans are very soft. Remove and discard the bay leaves. Remove the ham hocks from the pot, trim away fat and discard, cut lean meat away from the bone, chop coarsely, and return it to the pot. Stir and allow the meat to warm through before ladling soup in the bowls.

6 servings

SWEET POTATO, LEEK, AND SMOKED PORK SOUP

10	cups unsalted chicken broth		6	medium sweet potatoes, peeled and cooked
2	large smoked pork chops			Salt and white pepper to taste
8	slices of bacon, coarsely diced			
4	leeks (white part only), cleaned and trimmed			

Bring broth to a boil in a large kettle or pot. While broth is coming to a boil, trim any excess fat from smoked pork chops and rinse under cold, running water. Add chops to kettle and bring to a second boil. Reduce heat, cover, and simmer for 1 hour. While meat is simmering, fry bacon pieces until crisp and remove from the pot with a slotted spoon and place on a paper towel-lined plate to drain. Sauté leeks in bacon drippings until they are slightly transparent and use slotted spoon to remove them to the plate with the bacon pieces.

Remove the pork chops from the pot and, when they are sufficiently cool to handle, remove the meat from the bones, discard bones, and coarsely chop meat. Purée the sweet potatoes, leeks, bacon pieces, and chopped meat in a food processor in batches. Add broth to puree as necessary. Return purée to pot with broth. Season to taste, bring to a boil, reduce heat, and simmer for 20 minutes.

6 to 8 servings

HAM, POTATO, AND LEEK SOUP

Build a roaring fire in the fireplace, curl up with this soup, a favorite afghan, and a good book, and enjoy!

1	medium onion, finely chopped	1	ham bone
3	medium-size leeks (white part), minced	8	cups chicken broth
¼	cup leeks (light green part), minced	3	large potatoes, peeled and cubed
2	tablespoons butter	1½	cups whole kernel corn
		2	cups heavy cream
		3	cups coarsely chopped ham
			Salt and pepper to taste

In a large kettle or soup pot, sauté onion and leek whites in butter until they are slightly transparent, approximately 5 to 7 minutes; add leek greens, ham bone, and broth. Bring mixture to a boil, cover and simmer 2 hours. Remove bone from the kettle and, when it is sufficiently cool to handle, remove the meat from it. Discard bone, coarsely chop meat and return it to the pot. Add potatoes, bring to a second boil, and cook until potatoes are fork tender, approximately 5 to 7 minutes. Add corn, cream, chopped ham, and salt and pepper to taste.

8 servings

BAKED POTATO SOUP

5	slices of bacon	2	cups chicken broth
1	small onion, coarsely chopped	1	teaspoon salt
4	cups unpeeled baking potatoes, sliced	2	cups milk
1	teaspoon fresh parsley, minced	1¼	cups half-and-half
		1	cup Cheddar cheese
			Sour cream, chopped chives, and Cheddar cheese for garnish

In a large kettle or soup pot, fry bacon until crisp and then remove to a paper towel–lined plate to drain. Sauté onion in bacon drippings. Add next 5 ingredients and cook over medium-high heat, stirring often to prevent scorching. Cook 30 minutes or until the potatoes are fork tender. Place soup in blender and cream in two or more batches. Return to pot, add half-and-half and Cheddar cheese, and heat through without boiling. Serve in individual bowls. Garnish with additional cheese, a dollop of sour cream, crumbled bacon, and chives.

4 to 6 servings

Night scene of Howard University's campus
(Photograph courtesy Howard University Archives)

Gabrielle Kirk McDonald

[Judge Gabrielle Kirk McDonald] was one of the pioneer civil rights litigators in our country. And she has since become a pioneer justice for international war crimes law. . . . She will continue to be a voice for justice wherever she goes.

—Secretary of State Madeleine K. Albright,
Remarks honoring Judge McDonald as recipient
of the Leadership Award from the Central Eastern European Law Initiative

Gabrielle Kirk McDonald was born on April 12, 1942, in St. Paul, Minnesota, and spent her youth in Manhattan and Teaneck, New Jersey. She attended Boston University and Hunter College in New York before being admitted to Howard University Law School, where she was one of four women in her class. In 1966 she graduated first in her class.

McDonald then joined the NAACP Legal Defense and Educational Fund, where for three years she assisted plaintiffs and lawyers with issues relating to school desegregation, equal employment, housing, and voting rights. As the lead NAACP staff attorney, she filed a suit against Philip Morris Companies, Inc., for discriminatory practices, delivering the first significant plaintiff's victory under Title VII of the 1964 Civil Rights Act.

In 1969 she left the Legal Defense Fund to join her husband, Mark McDonald, in private practice in Houston. Together they successfully pursued plaintiff discrimination cases against corporate and labor giants such as Union Carbide, Monsanto, and Diamond Shamrock. Their largest case involved a $1.2 million settlement with the Lone Star Steel Company for back wages owed to 400 black workers.

McDonald's exceptional skills were soon noticed by others of influence, and in 1978, Texas Senator Lloyd Bentson nominated her for a federal judgeship. In 1979, when President Jimmy Carter appointed her to a federal district bench in Houston, she became the first African-American woman in Texas to be appointed to a federal bench and only the third in the nation. During a high-profile case involving the harassment of immigrant Vietnamese shrimp fishermen by the Ku Klux Klan, she and her family received anonymous death threats and "one-way tickets" to Africa.

In 1988 McDonald left the bench to re-enter private practice and began teaching a course in administrative law at Texas Southern University Law School. In 1993, after accepting a teaching position at St. Mary's School of Law in San Antonio, Texas, McDonald was recommended for a judgeship on the International Criminal Tribunal for the former Yugoslavia, established by the United Nations to try serious violations of international humanitarian law.

As one of eleven candidates considered for twenty-two tribunal positions, McDonald's broad and relevant experience resulted in her receiving the highest number of votes from the UN General Assembly, making her the only American on the court and one of only two women. From September to October of 1993 she taught full-time while drafting the proposed rules of procedure and evidence for the tribunal. McDonald served as presiding judge in the tribunal's Trial Chamber II and conducted its first trial.

Anthony Cassese, the tribunal's first president, described McDonald as "the best that America can offer . . . straightforward, direct, intelligent, and hard-working." After her election to a second term on the tribunal, McDonald was nominated and endorsed as president and presiding judge for the next two years.

A frequent lecturer on the work of the tribunal, Judge McDonald now serves as special counsel on human rights to the chairman of the board of directors of Freeport-McMoRan Copper & Gold Inc. Her many awards include: First Equal Justice Award, National Bar Association; nomination, Distinguished Alumni, Howard University; Doctor of Laws Honoris Causa, Georgetown University, 1993; Texas Women's Hall of Fame, 1993; Ronald Brown International Law Award, National Bar Association, 1997; Doctor of Laws Honoris Causa, Stetson College of Law, 1997; Goler Teal Butcher Award for Human Rights.

As we close this century, there is for the first time realistic hope of a more just future. A century stained with the sufferings of ceaseless war and atrocity is as much marked by our incomplete efforts to secure the foundations of an international society, one in which all peoples are equal and equally protected from abuse. . . . A properly functioning permanent court will be humanity's best chance yet to move out of its self-destructive cycle. Justice is a vindication, an historical right and a deterrent.

—Judge Gabrielle Kirk McDonald,
Past President of the International Criminal Tribunal for the former Yugoslavia,
to the Preparatory Commission for the International Criminal Court

WILD RICE, ROASTED CHICKEN, AND MUSHROOM SOUP

This elegant soup is as easy as it is delicious. Serve it with a crisp green salad and crusty bread for an unforgettable meal.

2 tablespoons butter	Bay leaf
1 cup onion, chopped	½ cup sliced mushrooms
½ cup celery, chopped	½ cup heavy cream
2 carrots, coarsely chopped	1¼ cups roasted chicken, coarsely
1½ cups uncooked wild rice	chopped
8¼ cups chicken broth	Salt and pepper to taste
¼ teaspoon dried rosemary	1 tablespoon sherry
leaves	Sliced green onions, including tops

Melt the butter in a large pot over medium-high heat. Add onion, celery, and carrots, reduce heat to medium, and sauté for 5 to 10 minutes or until the onion is limp and translucent. Add rice and stir to coat with butter. Add chicken broth, rosemary, and bay leaf, bring to a boil, reduce heat, and simmer for 1 hour or until the rice is tender. Add mushrooms during last 15 minutes of cooking time. Stir occasionally to prevent scorching. Add heavy cream and chicken, stir well, and allow to heat through before adding salt and pepper to taste. Stir in sherry and serve garnished with sliced green onions.

6 servings

HEARTY CORN AND CHICKEN CHOWDER

This robust soup will warm you on the coldest winter day!

¼	cup salt pork, cubed		1½	cups cooked chicken (bone and skin removed), coarsely chopped
1	large onion, chopped		1	large can evaporated milk
1	cup celery, chopped		1	12-ounce can whole kernel corn
2	large unpeeled potatoes, washed and cubed		1	16-ounce can cream-style corn
4	cups chicken broth			Chopped parsley to garnish
1	teaspoon salt			

Sauté salt pork in a Dutch oven until lightly browned. Add onion and celery; sauté until soft. Stir in potatoes and chicken broth. Cover and cook over medium- to medium-high heat until potatoes are fork tender. Add salt, chicken, evaporated milk, corn, and cream-style corn. Cook soup for an additional 10 minutes, or until it is warmed through. Serve garnished with minced parsley.

4 to 6 servings

Andrew Young

Andrew Young, an ordained minister, civil rights leader, former United Nations ambassador, mayor, and congressman, is one of the most influential and respected men of his generation. As a top aide to Dr. Martin Luther King, Jr., during the civil rights movement, he dedicated his life to the cause of equality and human rights.

Andrew Jackson Young, Jr., was born in New Orleans, Louisiana, on March 12, 1932. His father was a dentist and his mother a teacher. Following high school graduation, Young attended Dillard University in New Orleans for a year before transferring to Howard, where he graduated in 1951 at age 19. He then attended Hartford Theological Seminary, graduating with a B.D. in 1955.

While pastor of a church in Marion, Alabama, Young met and married Jean Childs, the daughter of a parishioner. During this period, he became deeply influenced by the teachings of Mohandas Gandhi and increasingly aware of the importance of the vote. He was working, despite threats to his life by white supremacists, to advance voter registration when he was introduced to Dr. Martin Luther King. The two found they had much in common (including membership in Alpha Phi Alpha, a black collegiate fraternity founded at Howard University) and they quickly became fast friends.

In 1957, Young accepted a position in New York City with the National Council of Churches, and in 1962 he resigned and moved to Atlanta, Georgia, where he continued his voter registration work. In 1964, Young became executive director of the Southern Christian Leadership Conference (SCLC), an organization formed by King and other African-American ministers to work for equal rights for African-Americans. Young organized peaceful protests, helped to write the Civil Rights Act of 1964, and participated in the historic civil rights march from Selma to Montgomery, Alabama, which ultimately led to the enactment of the Voting Rights Act of 1965. As a part of his work with the SCLC, Young assisted in negotiating the language of the Civil Rights Act of 1967, a law addressing the equal housing rights of African-Americans.

In 1968, following the assassination of Dr. King, Young made an unsuccessful bid for Congress. In 1972, undeterred, he won his bid to represent Georgia's Fifth Congressional District, becoming the first African-American elected from Georgia since 1871. Reelected in 1974 and 1976, Young's work on Jimmy Carter's campaign brought millions of new voters to the polls, tipping the electoral scales in Carter's favor. When Carter appointed him ambassador to the United Nations, Young became the first African-American to hold this position. He continued to champion the rights of the less powerful, and his strong anti-apartheid position brought criticism from the State Department, which eventually led to his resignation.

Elected mayor of Atlanta in 1991, and reelected to a second term in 1995, as part of the mayoralty Young was co-chairman of the Atlanta Committee for the Olympic Games. Today, through his consulting firm Good Works, which promotes positive business involvement in the U.S. and abroad, Andrew Young remains devoted to human rights.

The long walk
Howard students on the quadrangle.
(Private collection)

CHICKEN, RICE, AND TOMATO SOUP

Nothing says "welcome home" on a cold winter's day like the heartwarming fragrance of homemade soup. This is one of my favorites.

3½ to 4 pounds of chicken breasts, rib meat attached	1 cup raw, long-grain rice
3 quarts unsalted chicken broth	2 small tomatoes, peeled, seeded, and chopped
1¼ cups onion, chopped	2 tablespoons fresh flat-leafed parsley, minced
3 large celery ribs, sliced crosswise	1 teaspoon salt
3 large carrots, sliced to a thickness of ¼-inch	Freshly ground pepper

Wash chicken under cold running water, remove giblets, and reserve for another use. Combine chicken and broth in a 5-quart pot. Bring to a quick boil; reduce heat to medium, and cook for 15 minutes, skimming foam and fat off as needed.

Add next 4 ingredients, mix well, and bring to a second boil; reduce heat to medium-low, cover, and allow soup to simmer for 45 minutes. Transfer chicken to a large plate to cool. When it is sufficiently cool to handle remove and discard skin and bones. Coarsely chop meat and return to soup. Add remaining ingredients and heat soup through for an additional 5 minutes before serving.

8 to 10 servings

BEEF OKRA SOUP

1½ pounds beef stew	3 large tomatoes, peeled, seeded, and coarsely chopped
Salt and pepper to taste	1 cup cooked butter beans (canned is okay)
5 slices bacon	3 cups fresh okra, sliced
1 large onion, chopped	1½ quarts unsalted beef broth
1 beef shank bone	

Wash beef under cold running water, drain, salt and pepper to taste, and set aside. In a 3-quart pot, fry bacon over medium-high heat until it is crisp. Remove bacon from pot, add beef, and brown; add onion and continue to cook for an additional 5 minutes, stirring to prevent scorching. Add shank bone and water to cover by 1 inch. Bring to a quick boil, reduce heat to medium-low, cover and continue to simmer for 2½ hours. Add water as needed to prevent scorching. Add remaining ingredients and cook, uncovered, an additional 10 to 15 minutes or until okra is cooked through. Serve over a bed of rice for a great meal in a bowl.

4 to 6 servings

BEEF AND PASTA SHELL SOUP

1	pound cubed stew beef		5¾	cups unsalted beef broth
	Salt and pepper to taste		1	tablespoon tomato paste
1	tablespoon vegetable oil		1	cup frozen corn
1¼	cup onion, chopped		½	cup carrots, chopped
¾	cup celery, chopped		½	cup frozen peas
1	small clove garlic, minced		1	cup small pasta shells

Wash beef under cold running water and pat dry. Season the meat with salt and pepper to taste and set aside. In a large pot over medium-high heat, add vegetable oil and heat until a drop of water placed in the pot dances. Brown the meat for 4 minutes before adding onion, celery, and garlic. Continue to cook the meat and stir an additional 3 minutes, or until it is brown on all sides. Add the broth and tomato paste; mix well. Add corn, carrots, and peas. Bring mixture to a quick boil, reduce heat, and simmer for 30 minutes. Add additional broth or water as necessary to prevent scorching. Add pasta during the last 15 minutes of cooking time and simmer until the pasta is cooked through.

6 servings

Students socializing
(Private collection)

The Selma to Montgomery March:
A Long Walk to Voting Rights and Equality

In 1963, Selma, Alabama, was a small town where only 1 percent of eligible blacks were registered to vote. Many blacks, despite being more highly educated than the voting registrars, were unable to pass the voter registration test. Amelia Platts Boynton, a black Selma resident and civil rights activist, recalled that once when the test was administered to a black schoolteacher the registrar, apparently experiencing difficulty with pronunciation, was corrected by the teacher who finally said, "Those words are 'constitutionality' and 'interrogatory.'" The obviously embarrassed registrar "failed" the teacher and refused her registration.

Intimidation was also a means of dissuading blacks from attempting to register to vote. When SNCC organized voter registration events such as "Freedom Day" on October 7, 1963, a local photographer was ordered by Sheriff Jim Clark to take photographs of those attempting to register and ask what their employers would think of the pictures. If that tactic failed, police resorted to arrests or the brutal beating of SNCC workers and those they attempted to register.

At one such event, the sheriff arrested Amelia Boynton, who was well-respected in the community, roughly shoving her to the ground, then toward a waiting cruiser. On January 22, 1965, the arrest was protested by more than 100 schoolteachers, who marched to the courthouse. Inspired by their teachers' example, students joined the protest.

In a shocking turn of events, on February 18, 1965, Jimmy Lee Jackson, a black Vietnam veteran, his mother and grandfather were taking part in voter registration protests. When Jackson attempted to go to the aid of his mother and grandfather who were being beaten with billy clubs, he was shot by a state trooper and died seven days later. Following Jackson's death, plans were made for a march from Selma to Montgomery, fifty-four miles away. On Sunday, March 7, 1965, marchers starting across Selma's Edmund Pettus Bridge were met by police and state troopers. Under the orders of Governor George Wallace to stop the march, law enforcement officials issued the following warning: "It would be detrimental to your safety to continue this march. You are ordered to disperse, go home or to your church. This march will not continue." When the protesters refused to abandon the march, they were attacked. Tear gas was fired into the crowd and the protesters were severely beaten. Amelia Boynton, among the first marchers to cross the bridge, received blows so severe that her friends pulled her away thinking she was dead.

That night, regular television programming was interrupted to show clips of the violence at Selma. White citizens, some of whom had not been particularly concerned with the mounting racial injustice, were shocked by what they saw and called for restraint on the part of officials.

Dr. King, who had been preaching in Atlanta on "Bloody Sunday," as it was later called, rallied prominent people from around the nation to join in a second attempt to cross the bridge. The Alabama National Guard was federalized by President Johnson to provide protection to the marchers. On March 21, two weeks after Bloody Sunday, the marchers successfully crossed the Edmund Pettus Bridge and continued on the now-famous five-day march to Montgomery, which entered that city 25,000 strong, including Martin Luther King, Rosa Parks, John Lewis, and a host of Howard University graduates and students, among them Dr. Ralph Bunche, Andrew Young, James Farmer, and Stokely Carmichael.

The heroic efforts of the Selma marchers in the face of brutality and in full view of the media virtually guaranteed passage of the Voting Rights Act, which President Johnson signed on August 6, 1965. Voter registration among African-Americans in America rose from 21 percent in 1964 to 61 percent in 1969.

While blacks were not yet at the end of their long walk, they'd made significant strides.

SCALLOP AND LOBSTER CHOWDER

3   tablespoons butter
2   large onions, finely chopped
8   large unpeeled new potatoes, quartered
4½ cups clam juice
¼   teaspoon basil
1   small bay leaf
1   tablespoon chopped chives
1   pound small scallops, washed, drained, and coarsely chopped

1   pound lobster meat, coarsely chopped
2½ cups half-and-half
2½ cups milk
2   teaspoons salt
½   teaspoon white pepper
½   teaspoon paprika
⅛   teaspoon saffron
    Pinch of cayenne pepper

Melt butter in a 2½-quart kettle and sauté onions until they are tender and transparent. Add potatoes, clam juice, basil, bay leaf, and chives. Bring this mixture to a quick boil, reduce heat, cover, and cook over medium- to medium-low heat until potatoes are fork tender, approximately 15 to 20 minutes. Add scallops and lobster meat to the potato mixture and stir to blend. Add half-and-half, milk, and seasonings. Cover pot and bring to a second boil. Reduce heat to low and simmer gently for 5 additional minutes.

4 to 6 servings

Elaine R. Jones

The daughter of a Pullman porter and a schoolteacher, Elaine R. Jones graduated with honors in political science from Howard University. She then joined the Peace Corps and was one of the first African-Americans to serve in Turkey. At the conclusion of her two-year commitment, she entered the University of Virginia School of Law and was its first African-American woman graduate.

Jones joined the NAACP Legal Defense Fund to fight for equal rights and justice for people of color, women, and the poor. Only two years out of law school, she was the attorney of record in *Furman v. Georgia,* a landmark U.S. Supreme Court case that abolished the death penalty in thirty-seven states for twelve years. She also served as the legislative advocate in the Washington, D.C., NAACP office and played a key role in securing passage of the Voting Rights Act Amendments of 1982, the Fair Housing Act of 1988, the Civil Rights Restoration Act of 1988, and the Civil Rights Act of 1991.

In 1993, Jones became the first woman president and director-counsel of the NAACP Legal Defense and Educational Fund. In recognition of her leadership in the struggle for equality, she has earned numerous awards and honors, including the Eleanor Roosevelt Human Rights Award, presented by President Bill Clinton. In 2001, she was listed by *Ebony* magazine as one of the Ten Most Powerful Black Women and 100+ Most Influential Black Americans.

SHRIMP, OYSTER, AND CORN CHOWDER

3	tablespoons butter		¼	teaspoon thyme
2	large onions, finely chopped		⅛	teaspoon saffron
4½	cups clam juice			Pinch of cayenne pepper
1	small bay leaf		2	cups corn, drained
2½	cups half-and-half		2	pounds small fresh oysters, shucked
2½	cups milk		2	pounds medium shrimp
2	teaspoons salt			Chopped chives for garnish
½	teaspoon white pepper			
½	teaspoon paprika			

Melt butter in a 2½-quart kettle and sauté onions until they are limp and transparent. Add clam juice and bay leaf. Bring this mixture to a quick boil, reduce heat to medium or medium-low, cover, and cook approximately 15 to 20 minutes. Add half-and-half, milk, and seasonings. Cover pot and bring to a second boil. Add corn, oysters, and shrimp, stir to blend. Reduce heat to low and simmer gently for 5 additional minutes. Garnish with chopped chives prior to serving.

6 servings

OYSTER SOUP

1	quart freshly shucked oysters		1	tablespoon parsley, finely chopped
1	quart half-and-half		1	teaspoon onion juice
2	tablespoons butter			Salt and pepper to taste

Strain oysters, retaining juice, and remove any pieces of shell or other foreign objects from the oysters or their juice. Heat oyster juice, but do not allow it to boil. Add half-and-half to the oyster juice and stir. Add butter, parsley, and onion juice. Bring mixture to a simmer but do not boil. Add oysters one by one and salt and pepper to taste. When oysters puff and their edges crinkle, they are done. Serve immediately.

4 servings

CHUNKY CLAM CHOWDER IN A BREAD BOWL

Excellent when served with a crisp garden salad and a refreshing glass of white wine.

3 slices salt back bacon, cubed	4 6-ounce cans chopped clams, with liquid
5 tablespoons butter, divided	2 tablespoons butter
1¾ cups onion, chopped	Salt and pepper to taste
¾ cup celery, chopped	½ cup water
2 tablespoons flour	2 cups milk
5 large red potatoes, unpeeled and coarsely diced	2½ cups heavy cream
1 teaspoon whole thyme, dried (powdered can be used also)	1 cup bottled clam juice
	6 soup bowl–size rounds of bread
	Minced fresh parsley

Place the salt back bacon cubes in a large pot and brown over medium-high heat. Remove the bacon from the pot, leaving drippings in pot; melt 3 tablespoons of the butter in drippings. Add onions and celery, sauté until the onions are translucent and the celery is tender. Add flour, stir, and cook for 1 minute.

Add potatoes and thyme. Strain liquid from the clams into the pot (reserve clams and set aside), mix well, and add butter, salt, and pepper. Add water, reduce heat to medium and continue to cook over medium heat until potatoes are tender. Stir occasionally to prevent scorching. Add reserved clams, milk, heavy cream, bottled clam juice, remaining 2 tablespoons of butter, and cook an additional 5 minutes to allow the chowder to warm through.

A day in advance, or while soup is cooking, cut lids from 6 small rounds of bread. Hollow the middle to the size of a soup bowl and toast the bread. Cube the removed bread, brush with butter, and toast to use as soup croutons. If you prepare the bread bowls in advance, do not toast. Instead, cover the loaves with a tea towel and allow them to sit on the counter or in your oven to dry. Once again the rosemary bread is perfect for this dish as the rosemary in the bread imparts additional flavor to your chowder. Fill bowls with chowder and garnish with parsley.

6 servings

Patricia Roberts Harris

This country cannot afford either overt or subtle appeals to prejudice and hostility. We cannot risk the coming of a day when the United States turns to the world a face distorted by injustice condoned. Nor can we delude ourselves and our allies (for we will not delude our enemies) by insisting that there are easy solutions to international problems. We have a duty to continue the programs, domestic and international, which will result in justice, prosperity, and peace.

—Patricia Roberts Harris,
from the seconding address for the nomination of Lyndon B. Johnson
for president at the 1964 National Democratic Convention

Lawyer, educator, diplomat, public official, and civil rights activist, Patricia Harris distinguished herself in each vocation, and her many achievements included several "firsts," among them: the first black female cabinet member, first black female ambassador, first black female to serve in the United Nations, first black female on major corporate boards, first black female to chair a national political party committee, first black female to participate in a presidential nomination, first female to serve as dean of a law school, and first black, and only woman, to serve in three cabinet-level positions. Therefore it is not surprising that a U.S. commemorative stamp honors the achievements of this tireless supporter of civil rights initiatives and promoter of peace and justice for all.

Harris, a native of Mattoon, Illinois, earned her bachelor's from Howard in 1945, graduating Phi Beta Kappa and summa cum laude. While at Howard, she was active in the civil rights movement, participating in student demonstrations in Washington, D.C., which sought to desegregate segregated eating establishments. It was also at Howard that Patricia Roberts met her future husband, Professor William Beasley Harris, whom she married in 1955.

With her husband's encouragement, Harris entered George Washington University Law School, where she earned a doctorate with honors in jurisprudence in 1960. She then served briefly as a trial attorney in the Criminal Division of the United States Department of Justice but soon returned to Howard University, this time as the associate dean of students.

She was active in Democratic politics, served on several federal civil rights commissions, and in 1963, President John F. Kennedy appointed her to co-chair the National Women's Committee for Civil Rights. In 1964 Harris gave the seconding address for Lyndon Johnson's nomination, and President Johnson later appointed her ambassador to Luxembourg. She returned to Howard in 1967 and in 1969 became dean of the law school.

In 1971 Harris was appointed to the directorship of IBM, the first African-American woman to serve as a director of a major U.S. corporation. In 1977 President Jimmy Carter nominated her as the Secretary of Housing and Urban Development (HUD). After repeated challenges by Republican senators, she confidently responded, "You do not seem to understand who I am. I am a black woman, the daughter of a dining car waiter. I am a black woman who could not buy a house eight years ago in parts of the District of Columbia." It seemed that they finally understood, because she was finally confirmed and became the first black woman to serve in a presidential cabinet. Two years later, she was named Secretary of Health and Human Services. While serving, Mrs. Harris secured additional funding for HUD and dramatically increased the availability of subsidized housing and grants to new businesses in blighted neighborhoods.

Patricia Roberts Harris left the federal government after Ronald Reagan's election, and in 1982 she ran an unsuccessful campaign against Marion Barry for mayor of Washington, D.C. On March 23, 1985, Mrs. Harris died following a battle with breast cancer. Part of her national legacy is the Patricia Roberts Harris Public Affairs Program at Howard University, a living memorial to an American trailblazer. The center was established in October 1987 to encourage students to consider careers in public service, and it offers public service internships in selected government offices and private organizations.

The Patricia Roberts Harris Public Affairs Program

The Harris Public Affairs Program in association with the Ralph J. Bunche International Affairs Center, grew out of a bequest made to Howard by Patricia Roberts Harris. "Its purpose is twofold: to complement the university's course offerings in areas related to public policy, and to encourage students to consider careers in public service.

"Key features of the Harris Program include an annual lecture focusing on a major issue or issues of national and/or international concern, and the Visiting Fellows Program, which brings outstanding public affairs professionals to Howard to share informally their expertise with students." (www.huarchivesnet.ed)

Golden anniversary

Patricia Roberts Harris, first national executive of Delta Sigma Theta sorority, greets Vice President Lyndon Baines Johnson and his wife, Ladybird, at the sorority's golden anniversary celebration as university president, James Nabrit looks on. (*Photograph courtesy Howard University Archives*)

In addition, the Harris Program facilitates international travel and study opportunities and sponsors internships for Howard University students, providing a firsthand introduction to public service careers in Congress, in federal and District of Columbia agencies, and in private organizations concerned with public policy issues. In addition to serving in the Executive Office of the President, Harris Fellows have worked abroad in such places as the American embassy in Paris; the World Council of Churches in Geneva; and the American Consulate General in Durban, South Africa.

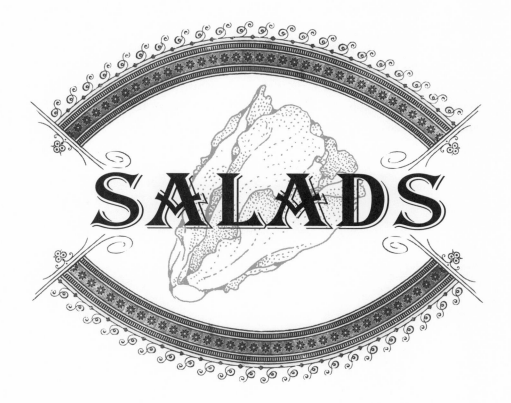

SALADS

Salad Notes: When preparing lettuce greens for a fresh green salad, first remove and discard wilted outer leaves and remove the core from the lettuce. You can either use a lettuce corer, or, with iceberg lettuce in particular, strike the flat end of the core hard against the kitchen counter and then remove the loosened core from the lettuce. After the core is removed, separate the leaves and inspect them for worms, etc. Rinse the greens in cold water, drain, and pat or spin dry before tearing into bite-size leaves. Tearing the leaves helps your salad greens to better absorb the salad dressing.

FRIED CHICKEN POTATO SALAD

For a soulful salad luncheon buffet, serve the fried chicken potato salad with the black-eyed pea, okra, and sweet potato salads—the recipes immediately follow.

7 pieces cold Spicy Fried Chicken (see recipe on page 179)*	1¼ teaspoons garlic, minced
1 cup mayonnaise	⅓ cup red bell pepper, minced
¼ cup sour cream	⅓ cup yellow bell pepper, minced
1 tablespoon spicy brown mustard	⅓ cup green onions, sliced
7 boiled eggs, riced	¾ cup sweet pickle relish
⅓ cup onions, minced	⅛ teaspoon cayenne pepper
⅓ cup celery, minced	7 cups potatoes, cooked and cubed
	Salt and pepper to taste

Debone and cube chicken, leaving the skin on. Set aside. In a large mixing bowl, combine mayonnaise, sour cream, and mustard, blending well. Rice eggs by firmly drawing a fork through whole eggs until crumbled. Add the riced eggs to the mixture. Combine all remaining ingredients except the chicken and potatoes, and mix well. Add potatoes, blending well into the mixture, and then gently toss in the cold fried chicken cubes. Season salad with salt and pepper to taste. Place on a large serving platter and garnish with boiled eggs, or surround the salad with additional pieces of hot, fried chicken.

8 to 10 servings

*If leftover fried chicken is unavailable, simply visit your favorite fried chicken fast food outlet and purchase 7 pieces of their spicy version.

Sharon Pratt Kelly

Sharon Pratt Kelly defied overwhelming odds to become the first African-American woman elected as mayor of a major American city, Washington, D.C. During her term from 1991 to 1995, Kelly's policies improved city finances, decreased crime, and developed programs for the city's deprived elderly and at-risk youth.

A Washington, D.C., native, Kelly earned her bachelor's with honors from Howard University in 1965 and her law degree from Howard in 1968. She entered private practice in 1971 and taught at the Antioch School of Law in Washington, D.C., from 1972 to 1976. She represented Washington, D.C., on the Democratic National Committee from 1977 to 1990, where she served as committee treasurer for four years. With the campaign slogan YES WE WILL and a promise to restore the city to its former greatness by "cleaning house" and effecting city-wide reforms, Kelly swept to mayoral victory on November 6, 1990. She has received numerous national awards for her political service, including the NAACP Award, the Thurgood Marshall Award of Excellence, and the Mary McLeod Bethune–W. E. B. DuBois Award, presented by the Congressional Black Caucus.

BLACK-EYED PEA SALAD

Enjoy black-eyed peas as a salad. This is certain to become a favorite at barbecues, fish fries, and picnics.

2	cans black-eyed peas, drained		1	ripe tomato, chopped
1	fresh jalapeño pepper, seeded and finely minced		1	teaspoon fresh parsley, minced
1	garlic clove, minced		3	garlic cloves, minced
¼	cup onion, finely chopped		⅔	cup olive oil
¼	cup yellow bell pepper, chopped		⅓	cup fresh lemon juice
¼	cup celery, chopped			Salt and freshly ground pepper to taste

Combine peas, jalapeño, garlic, onion, bell pepper, celery, and tomatoes, and mix well to blend. Next, make dressing by combining remaining ingredients in a screw-top jar. Cover and shake well to mix. Pour over salad and refrigerate 2 hours before serving.

6 servings

OKRA SALAD

1 pound fresh okra	1 large ripe tomato, diced into ½-inch pieces
2 cups buttermilk	1 small yellow onion, diced into ½-inch pieces
1 cup corn meal	1 small green bell pepper, seeded and diced into ½-inch pieces
1 cup self-rising flour	Salt and freshly ground pepper to taste
1 teaspoon salt	
¼ teaspoon ground red pepper	
8 slices bacon, coarsely chopped	
Vegetable oil	

Wash okra and then cut off and discard the tips and stems. Cut okra crosswise into ½-inch slices. Place in a glass or ceramic bowl, cover with buttermilk, and refrigerate for approximately 45 minutes to 1 hour. Meanwhile, combine cornmeal, flour, salt, and red pepper. Mix well. In a frying pan over medium-high heat, fry the bacon until crisp. Use a slotted spoon to transfer bacon to paper towel–lined plate to drain. Reserve the bacon drippings in the pan. If required, add vegetable oil to bacon drippings to reach a pan depth of 2 inches. Remove okra from the buttermilk with a slotted spoon, and discard the buttermilk. Toss the sliced okra in the cornmeal to coat evenly. Fry okra in small batches until golden brown and crisp tender, approximately 6 to 7 minutes. Turn as needed for even browning. Use a slotted spoon to transfer the okra to a paper towel–lined plate to drain. Transfer the okra to a bowl and add the tomato, onion, and bell pepper. Toss to mix. Add salt and pepper to taste and toss again. Garnish with crumbled bacon and serve immediately.

6 servings

SWEET POTATO SALAD

3   pounds sweet potatoes, unpeeled
1   cup corn
1   cup sweet red pepper, chopped
½   cup onion, chopped
1¼   cups mayonnaise
1½   teaspoons salt
¼   teaspoon Tabasco sauce
1   clove garlic, minced

1   fresh jalapeño pepper, seeded and minced
¼   cup fresh lime juice
1   teaspoon prepared Dijon-style mustard
2   teaspoons cumin
¼   teaspoon curry powder
2   tablespoons chopped cilantro
¼   teaspoon coarsely ground pepper

Choose firmer potatoes or your salad will be mushy. Boil potatoes in salted water until fork tender. Drain the potatoes and chill overnight. Peel sweet potatoes and dice into ½-inch cubes. Add corn, red peppers, and onions to potatoes. In a separate bowl combine remaining ingredients, gently blend into the potato mixture and add salt to taste.

8 servings

MIXED GREENS AND RED ONION SALAD

3   cups torn romaine lettuce
3   cups torn iceberg lettuce
2   cups baby spinach leaves (long stems removed)
1   cup watercress leaves
½   medium red onion, sliced thin and separated into rings

2   tablespoons sugar
⅓   cup white wine vinegar
½   cup vegetable oil
½   teaspoon dry mustard
2   hard-boiled eggs, peeled and crumbled
8   slices bacon, cooked crisp, drained, and crumbled

In a large salad or mixing bowl combine salad greens and onion rings. Refrigerate salad 20 to 30 minutes. In a screw-top jar combine sugar, white wine vinegar, vegetable oil, and dry mustard. Cover and shake well. Dress salad, garnish with eggs, cover tightly, and refrigerate 20 to 30 minutes prior to serving. Add crumbled bacon immediately before serving.

6 servings

HEARTS OF PALM, TOMATO, CUCUMBER, AND BLACK OLIVE SALAD

1	14-ounce can hearts of palm, drained and halved	½	cup extra-virgin olive oil
2	tomatoes, cut into wedges	3	tablespoons fresh lime juice
2	cucumbers, scored and sliced	½	teaspoon salt
¼	cup red onion, chopped	¼	teaspoon dry mustard
½	cup pitted black olive halves	1	small clove garlic, minced
		6	cups torn mixed salad greens

In a large salad or mixing bowl combine hearts of palm, tomatoes, cucumbers, onion, and black olives. Next, in a screw-top jar, combine extra-virgin olive oil, lime juice, salt, dry mustard, and minced garlic. Cover tightly and shake well to mix. Pour over vegetables and refrigerate several hours before serving. Use a slotted spoon to strain vegetable mixture from the dressing and place on individual beds of salad greens.

6 servings

SPRING GARDEN TOSSED SALAD

Recently my husband and I were dining at the Sheppard Air Force Base Officer's Club. Dinner was delicious. However, I was particularly intrigued with the salad. The chef, "Big Ed," substituted seedless grapes for the cherry tomatoes called for below. While they had the texture and consistency of cherry tomatoes, they provided a sweet surprise for the palate.

3 cups torn romaine lettuce	1 cup cherry tomatoes, halved
3 cups torn iceberg lettuce	1 tablespoon fresh parsley, minced
1 cup torn curly endive lettuce	3 garlic cloves, minced
2 tablespoons parsley, minced	⅔ cup olive oil
1½ cups carrot, thinly sliced	⅓ cup fresh lemon juice
½ cup celery, coarsely chopped	¾ cup bleu cheese, crumbled
½ cup radish, thinly sliced	
4 green onions, including tops, sliced thin	

In a large salad or mixing bowl combine lettuces, parsley, carrot, celery, radish, green onions, and cherry tomatoes. Next, make dressing by combining parsley, garlic, olive oil, and lemon juice in a screw-top jar. Cover and shake well to mix. Refrigerate salad dressing and salad greens 20 to 30 minutes before serving. Dress salad and garnish with bleu cheese just prior to serving.

6 servings

David Norman Dinkins

David Norman Dinkins was born on July 10, 1927, in Trenton, New Jersey, where he and his family lived until the Depression forced them to move to Harlem.

After serving overseas in the Marines during World War II, Dinkins entered college and received his B.S. in mathematics from Howard University in 1950. After graduating from Brooklyn Law School in 1956, he entered private practice until 1975, when he became president of the New York City Board of Elections. He became president of the Borough of Manhattan in 1985 and was elected mayor in 1989, the first African-American to hold that office in New York City.

Garden party
The occasion was hosted by the Dean of Women in honor of the women members of the class of 1953.
(Photograph courtesy Howard University Archives)

TOSSED GREEN SALAD

This simple garden salad is excellent with grilled steak or chicken.

2	cloves garlic, mashed		1	cup pitted black olive halves
¾	cup olive oil		1	cucumber, scored and sliced
2	cups homemade croutons *(see below)*		½	small Bermuda onion, sliced thin
1	small head iceberg lettuce		1	teaspoon salt
1	small head romaine lettuce		⅓	cup fresh lemon juice
				Freshly grated Parmesan cheese

Combine garlic and olive oil in a small bowl and allow to stand several hours or overnight. Wash, drain, and pat or spin lettuce dry; refrigerate at least one hour before preparing salad. Tear lettuce into bite-size pieces and add to the salad bowl, along with black olives, cucumber, and Bermuda onion. Remove the garlic from the olive oil. Combine the garlic-flavored oil with salt and lemon juice. Dress salad to coat and garnish with croutons and Parmesan to taste just before serving.

6 servings

HOMEMADE CROUTONS

Crunchy homemade croutons really add zest to a simple green garden salad. These croutons are a family favorite. I hope you enjoy them as much as we do!

ITALIAN HERB CROUTONS

3	cups 1- to 1½-inch cubes day-old Cuban, Italian, or French bread		1	tablespoon butter
3	tablespoons extra-virgin olive oil		3	large cloves garlic, minced
			¼	teaspoon dried rosemary, crushed
			1	teaspoon Italian seasoning herbs

Place bread cubes in a large mixing bowl and set aside. In a large skillet heat oil and butter over medium-low heat until the butter melts. Add garlic and seasonings; cook 5 or 6 minutes. Remove skillet from heat and drizzle melted oil mixture over the croutons while stirring to evenly coat. Toast cubes in skillet over medium-low heat until cubes are lightly browned and crisp. Remove from pan and drain on paper towels. Croutons may be stored in a tightly covered container for up to one week.

Yields 3 cups

GARLIC CROUTONS

3 cups 1- to 1½-inch cubes day-old Cuban, Italian, or French bread	3 tablespoons extra-virgin olive oil 1 tablespoon butter 4 large cloves garlic, minced

Place bread cubes in a large mixing bowl and set aside. Place oil and butter in a large skillet and heat over a medium-low flame until the butter melts. Add garlic to the skillet and cook 5 or 6 minutes. Remove skillet from heat and drizzle melted oil mixture over the croutons while stirring to evenly coat. Toast cubes in skillet over medium-low heat until cubes are lightly browned and crisp. Remove from pan and drain on paper towels. Croutons may be stored in a tightly covered container for up to one week.

Yields 3 cups

FRUIT SALAD

3 cups strawberries, washed, hulled, and halved
3 cups green seedless grapes
1 cup fresh blueberries
1 cantaloupe, removed from shell, seeded, and cut into bite-size chunks

1 honeydew melon, removed from shell, seeded, and cut into bite-size chunks
Fresh mint leaves

Combine above ingredients in a serving bowl, add dressing (recipe follows), cover, and refrigerate at least one hour. Mix well before serving. Garnish with fresh mint leaves.

6 to 8 servings

DRESSING

⅓ cup sherry
½ cup powdered sugar

2 tablespoons Madeira

Combine the above ingredients, mix well, and dress salad.

Yields approximately ¾ cup

COUNTRY COLE SLAW

5 cups cabbage, shredded
1¼ cups carrots, shredded
¼ cup onion, finely chopped
½ cup mayonnaise
2 tablespoons buttermilk
1 tablespoon sugar

1 tablespoon vinegar
½ teaspoon salt
Dash of pepper
½ teaspoon caraway seed
½ teaspoon celery seed

Combine cabbage, carrots, and onion in a large serving bowl and set aside. Combine remaining ingredients in a separate bowl and stir until sugar completely dissolves. Add to cabbage mixture and toss to coat. Cover and thoroughly chill for approximately 1 hour before serving.

6 to 8 servings

Graduation at Howard University
(Private collection)

DILLED DELI POTATO SALAD

15	small red potatoes (approximately 1½ pounds)	1	teaspoon sugar
½	cup onion, finely chopped	½	teaspoon salt
¾	cup mayonnaise	3	teaspoons fresh dill, minced
2	tablespoons fresh lemon juice	2	tablespoons water

Boil potatoes in sufficient water to cover and allow them to boil freely. While potatoes are boiling, combine remaining ingredients and refrigerate. When potatoes are fork tender, drain away water and remove potatoes from the pot. After potatoes are sufficiently cool to handle, peel and slice them thin. Dress with mayonnaise mixture, combine well and chill for approximately 1 hour before serving.

6 to 8 servings

PALATE-PLEASING PASTA SALAD

1	7-ounce package seashell pasta, cooked	1	cucumber, peeled, seeded, and cut into large cubes
6	ounces provolone cheese, cut into ¾-inch cubes	¼	cup freshly grated Parmesan cheese
½	cup green onion, (including tops), sliced	¼	cup snipped fresh parsley
½	cup chopped sweet red pepper	1	small clove garlic, minced
2	2¼-ounce cans sliced pitted ripe olives, drained	⅓	cup olive oil
1	14-ounce can hearts of palm, drained and halved	¼	cup white wine vinegar
		1½	teaspoons dry mustard
		1	teaspoon dried oregano, crushed
		1	teaspoon dried basil, crushed
		2	medium tomatoes, cut into wedges
			Parsley sprigs (optional)

Cook pasta according to package directions; drain. Rinse with cold water and drain again. In a large mixing bowl combine pasta, provolone cheese, green onion, sweet red pepper, olives, hearts of palm, cucumber, Parmesan cheese, and snipped parsley.

In a screw-top jar combine garlic, olive oil, vinegar, dry mustard, oregano, and basil. Cover and shake well. Pour dressing over pasta mixture and toss lightly to coat. Transfer salad to a serving bowl. Cover and chill for at least 4 hours. The salad may be prepared up to this point 24 hours in advance. Just prior to serving, add tomato wedges and toss lightly. Garnish with parsley.

8 to 10 servings

TURKEY, WALNUT, AND APPLE SALAD

This salad is also delicious when served chilled in a croissant.

4 cups smoked turkey breast, diced	Up to ¼ teaspoon ground cumin to taste
⅓ cup green onions, sliced	3 cups Granny Smith apples, pared, cored, and coarsely chopped
1 cup celery, coarsely chopped	¾ cup chopped walnuts
½ cup sour cream	2 tablespoons olive oil
½ cup mayonnaise	1 tablespoon baker's sugar
¼ teaspoon salt	1 teaspoon ground cinnamon
⅛ teaspoon coarsely ground black pepper	

In a large salad or mixing bowl combine the turkey, onion, and celery and refrigerate. In a separate bowl, combine sour cream, mayonnaise, salt, pepper, cumin, and apple. Add mayonnaise mixture to the turkey mixture and mix well to combine. Return salad to the refrigerator to chill. While salad is chilling, sauté walnuts in olive oil until crisp, but not too dark or burnt. Transfer to a paper towel–lined plate to drain. Combine sugar and cinnamon and sprinkle walnuts with mixture before they cool. Use to garnish individual servings of salad.

6 servings

GREAT CAESAR'S MEDITERRANEAN CHICKEN SALAD

2   cloves garlic, pressed
2   tablespoons fresh lemon juice
1   teaspoon dried oregano
½   teaspoon salt
⅓   cup extra-virgin olive oil
3   cups smoked chicken breast, thinly sliced
1   cup kalamata olives, halved

1   7-ounce can artichoke hearts, drained and halved
½   cup pepperoncini peppers
1   cup red onion, thinly sliced
5   cups torn romaine lettuce, chilled
5   ounces crumbled feta cheese
½   cup Garlic Croutons (page 121)

First, make dressing by whisking together garlic, lemon juice, dried oregano, and salt. Slowly whisk in extra-virgin olive oil. Combine chicken, olives, artichoke hearts, peppers, and onions. Combine with ¼ cup of the salad dressing and gently mix to evenly coat. Coat the romaine lettuce with remaining dressing. Divide dressed lettuce among 4 salad plates, top with chicken mixture and feta. Garnish salad with Garlic Croutons.

4 servings

WARM PECAN CHICKEN SALAD

½   cup pecan halves
8   tablespoons olive oil, divided
1   cup red onion, sliced and separated into rings
1   pound skinless, boneless chicken breasts (approximately 3)

½   teaspoon salt
½   teaspoon black pepper
1½ tablespoons red wine vinegar
2   tablespoons sour cream
¼   pound Roquefort cheese
8   ounces baby spinach leaves, long stems removed

In a large skillet, toast pecans over moderately low heat, stirring frequently until pecans are golden brown, approximately 5 minutes. Remove nuts from the pan and set aside. In the same pan, add 1 tablespoon of oil to skillet and sauté onions over high heat for 2 minutes until light in color and crisp tender. Remove onions from the skillet and add to the plate with the pecans. Add 2 tablespoons of oil to the pan and heat over a moderate burner. Combine salt and pepper and use mixture to season chicken breasts to taste. Place chicken breasts in the pan and brown, approximately 4 minutes on each side. Cover the pan so that steam does not escape, and allow to sit undisturbed for 5 minutes. Remove the chicken breasts from the pan and, when they are sufficiently cool to handle, cut them into bite-size pieces. If chicken is not cooked through, return it to the pan and sauté over medium-high heat until done.

While chicken is cooling, whisk together the vinegar and sour cream in a glass or stainless-steel bowl. Add the remaining 5 tablespoons of oil to the mixture in a slow, steady stream. Add Roquefort and stir just to combine, leaving the dressing chunky. Return chicken to pan and reduce heat to low. Add salad dressing and stir until chicken is coated. Remove from heat. Arrange spinach on four individual serving plates. Top with chicken, onions, and pecans.

4 servings

CURRIED CHICKEN SALAD

4 cups cooked chicken, cut into chunks	⅔ cup sour cream
2 cups seedless grapes, halved	2 teaspoons curry powder
⅔ cup mayonnaise	2 cups cashews, coarsely chopped
	Lettuce

Place chicken and grapes in mixing bowl. Next, in a separate bowl, combine mayonnaise, sour cream, and curry powder; stir until well blended. Pour over chicken mixture and mix well to thoroughly coat. Chill 1 hour; stir in cashews and gently blend immediately before serving so that they remain crisp and serve on a bed of crisp green lettuce leaves.

6 to 8 servings

SALMON AND POTATO SALAD

3   cups unpeeled red potatoes,
      cooked and quartered
4   hard-boiled egg whites,
      coarsely chopped (reserve
      yolks)
½   cup celery, thinly sliced
¼   cup green onion, thinly sliced
¼   cup yellow pepper, chopped
¼   cup red pepper, chopped

¼   cup green pepper, chopped
1½ cups heavy cream
¾   cup mayonnaise
¼   teaspoon salt
¼   teaspoon paprika
1   pound boneless skinless salmon,
      canned or fresh cooked
Salad greens

In a large salad or mixing bowl combine potatoes, egg whites, celery, green onion, and peppers. In a separate bowl whip cream until very stiff and fold in mayonnaise. Add salt and paprika; mix well and combine with the potato mixture until well blended. Gently fold in salmon chunks, cover, and chill thoroughly, approximately 1 hour. Serve on a crisp bed of salad greens and garnish with riced egg yolks.

6 servings

SALMON AND PASTA SALAD

1   pound boneless skinless
      salmon, canned or fresh
      cooked
3   cups cooked corkscrew pasta
4   hard-boiled eggs, coarsely
      chopped
2   cups cucumber, diced

⅓   cup red onion, chopped
¼   cup yellow pepper, chopped
¼   cup red pepper, chopped
¼   cup green pepper, chopped
¼   teaspoon salt
¼   teaspoon paprika
Vinaigrette Dressing

In a large salad or mixing bowl combine salmon, pasta, eggs, cucumber, red onion, and peppers. Combine salt and paprika. Add to salad and lightly toss. Dress with Vinaigrette Dressing (recipe opposite) and refrigerate at least 1 hour prior to serving with ½ cup of dressing or to taste.

6 servings

VINAIGRETTE DRESSING

⅔   cup vegetable oil
⅔   cup chicken broth
½   cup cider vinegar
2   small cloves garlic

2   teaspoons Dijon-style mustard
½   teaspoon salt
¾   teaspoon sugar

Process all ingredients in a blender or food processor until they are well blended. Pour salad dressing into a jar and cover tightly.

Yields approximately 2½ cups

Early sewing class at Howard University
(Corbis)

VEGETABLES

Howard University graduating class, c.1900
(Corbis)

A Hospital for Freedmen:
A Place of Healing that Began in War

On November 6, 1860, Abraham Lincoln, having run on the Republican Party's anti-slavery platform, was elected president of the United States. The southern states quickly began seceding from the Union: First was South Carolina, on December 20, 1860; and by the following February, six more—Mississippi, Florida, Alabama, Georgia, Louisiana, and Texas—had split from the Union. War ensued, and the Union was divided for four years.

Perhaps in an effort at reconciliation or simply as a matter of preservation, Lincoln's inaugural address proclaimed his duty to maintain the Union; at the same time he declared that he had no intention of ending existing slavery or repealing the Fugitive Slave Law. Despite his conciliatory attempts, on April 12 the Confederacy attacked Fort Sumter, a federal stronghold in Charleston, South Carolina.

When four more states seceded—Virginia, Arkansas, North Carolina, and Tennessee—Lincoln persisted in his position that the war's objective was not emancipation or black rights; but rather, preserving the Union. As one result, the government was forced to turn away African-American volunteers who had rushed to enlist. Some, bound by slavery, were eager to fight for their own freedom; others, already free, were ready to fight for loved ones still in bondage. African-Americans already serving on naval ships were permitted to continue their service, but Lincoln upheld the laws barring blacks from the United States Army, reassuring northern whites that they could be secure in the privileges of their race.

Some of those seeking to serve were fugitive slaves, and because President Lincoln had promised to uphold the Fugitive Slave Act, Union soldiers had the unusual duty of returning runaway slaves to their masters, who in turn often used them against the Union in the war effort. When three runaway slaves sought refuge at Fortress Monroe, the commanding colonel, Benjamin Franklin Butler, disregarded the Act to provide them a safe haven behind enemy lines. The secessionist owner sent an emissary to recover his "property" under the Fugitive Slave Act, but Butler responded that he was under no obligation to uphold the property rights of citizens of a foreign country.

In April of 1861, slavery was abolished in the District of Columbia. Consequently, as union troops advanced across the South, thousands of contraband and freed slaves began migrating to Washington, D.C. On January 1, 1863, President Lincoln emancipated all slaves held within states that were in rebellion and not in Union hands.

It was only after Lincoln issued the final Emancipation Proclamation that African-American soldiers were officially accepted into federal ranks. Two of those soldiers would immediately influence the lives of freedmen and significantly shape the future of Howard University.

Anderson R. Abbott

Born in Toronto, Canada, on April 7, 1837, Anderson Ruffin Abbott was the son of Wilson R. and Ellen Toyer Abbott, free people of color who had immigrated to Toronto from Mobile, Alabama, in 1835. Excelling in academics, Anderson was an honor student at the Toronto Academy, studied at Oberlin College in Ohio, and earned a medical degree from Trinity Medical College in 1861.

A friend and mentor to Abbott was Dr. Alexander T. Augusta, a freeborn black who had received his medical degree at Trinity in 1856. Augusta was commissioned in the U.S. Army in 1863 and that same year, his young protégée, Anderson Abbott, wrote to Secretary of War E. M. Stanton on February 6:

> *I learn by our city papers that it is the intention of the government of the United States to raise 150,000 coloured troops. Being one of that class, I beg to make application for a commission as assistant surgeon. My qualifications are that I am 24 years of age; I have studied medicine five years; I am a licentiate of the college of Physicians and Surgeons of Upper Canada . . . I am also a matriculant of the Toronto University. . . .*

His first letter apparently unanswered, on April 30, 1863, Abbott again wrote to Stanton.

> *Sir: I beg most respectfully to apply for a situation as medical cadet in the army. I am a coloured man, and would desire to be appointed in one of the coloured regiments, if you think favorably of my application.*
>
> *It may be some recommendation to add that I have been a pupil of Dr. A. T. Augusta for several years—he received a commission from you, as a surgeon, recently. He will give you all the information you may require concerning my character and attainments.*
>
> *Yours Respectfully, A. R. Abbott.*

According to National Archives records, Abbott was sworn in to the army as acting assistant surgeon on September 2, 1863, receiving a monthly sum of $100.00, except when serving in the field, when he received $113.83 and "transportation in kind." When Abbott got to Washington, it is likely that he was confronted with confusion and overcrowding caused by thousands of fugitives fleeing across Union lines to the District for protection. Unprepared for the deluge as hungry, ill-clothed, sick, and feeble former slaves, swept into the city, the government was unable to meet all of their needs. Private citizens, both black and white, stood in the gap, and taught the fugitives to read and write while at the same time attempting to attend to their medical needs.

After the announcement of emancipation in the District of Columbia, camps were established there to assist the freedmen. However, they were soon overpopulated and disease became common. A cluster of barracks began treating the refugees. Dr. Abbott served in the Washington, D.C., "contraband camp" from June 26, 1863, to June 25, 1864 and was a founder of Freedmen's Hospital, serving for a time as its chief executive officer. His outstanding skills and service were soon recognized and he was one of eight black physicians appointed to the Army Medical Corps. While serving in Washington, DC., both he and Dr. Augusta were warmly received by President and Mrs. Lincoln at a "soirée" to which the president had invited them. After Lincoln's assassination, Mrs. Lincoln presented Dr. Abbott with one of the president's plaid shawls as a memento.

The hospital founded as Freedmen's Hospital in 1862 developed into today's Howard University Hospital, a first-class medical facility. Its initial purpose was to provide health care for newly freed slaves faced with financial hardship and racial discrimination, and by 1868, the Freedmen's Hospital consisted of several small frame buildings located on the corner of 5th and W streets in Northwest Washington, D.C. Eventually, Freedmen's Hospital and the Howard University College of Medicine were consolidated to train African-American medical professionals.

In 1961, President John F. Kennedy signed legislation officially transferring the title of Freedmen's Hospital to Howard University, and in 1975 Howard University Hospital officially opened the doors of a 515-bed facility at its current location on Georgia Avenue, NW. Since its founding, Howard University has trained some of the world's foremost physicians, and as evidenced by its Cancer Center, Center for Sickle Cell Disease, and neonatal disease and minority organ transplant tissue education programs, Howard University Hospital is on the cutting edge of modern health-care research and delivery.

Freedmen's Hospital at Howard University
(Photograph courtesy Howard University Archives)

HOWARD HISTORY MAKER: Dr. LaSalle D. Leffall, Jr., is a world-renowned surgeon, oncologist, and medical educator. He graduated first in his class from the Howard University School of Medicine in 1953, and joined the Howard faculty as an associate professor of medicine in 1962. In 1970 he was named Charles R. Drew Professor, assuming the university's first endowed chair of surgery. Dr. Leffall has further distinguished himself as the first African-American president of four organizations: the American Cancer Society, the American College of Surgeons, the Society of Surgical Oncology, and the Society of Surgical Chairmen in the United States. In 2002, Dr. Leffall was appointed by President George W. Bush to chair the President's Cancer Panel. He is also chairman of the board of the Susan G. Komen Breast Cancer Foundation.

FRIED OKRA

Originating in present-day Ethiopia, the use of okra eventually spread throughout North Africa before coming to the new world. One of the earliest references to this plant was by a Spanish Moor who, while visiting Egypt in 1216, explained that the plants were eaten with corn meal when they were young and tender.

1 pound fresh okra	1 teaspoon salt
2 cups buttermilk	¼ teaspoon ground red pepper
1 cup corn meal	8 slices bacon, coarsely chopped
1 cup self-rising flour	Vegetable oil

Wash okra, then cut off and discard stems. Cut okra crosswise into ½-inch slices. Place in a nonreactive bowl, cover with buttermilk, and refrigerate for approximately 45 minutes to 1 hour. Meanwhile, combine cornmeal, flour, salt, and red pepper. Mix well. In a frying pan over medium heat, fry the bacon until crisp. Use a slotted spoon to transfer bacon to a paper towel–lined plate to drain. Reserve the bacon drippings in the pan. If required, add vegetable oil to bacon drippings to reach a pan depth of 2 inches. Remove okra from the buttermilk with a slotted spoon, and discard the buttermilk. Toss the sliced okra in the corn meal to coat evenly. Fry okra in small batches until golden brown and crisp tender, approximately 6 to 7 minutes. Turn as needed to ensure even browning. Using a slotted spoon, transfer the okra to a paper towel–lined plate to drain.

4 to 6 servings

TOMATOES AND OKRA

It is thought that slaves brought okra seeds with them to America. Thomas Jefferson indicated that they were found in Virginia as early as 1781. In America this African staple was also enjoyed fried in corn meal. However, it was also very popular with French colonists who used it in various ways, including stewed in *gumbo,* which is an African word for okra.

1 large sweet onion, coarsely chopped	2 tablespoons minced celery
¼ cup green pepper, chopped	1 pound fresh okra, cut crosswise in ½-inch slices
3 tablespoons bacon drippings	1 teaspoon salt
¼ teaspoon minced garlic	1 teaspoon pepper
3 large ripe tomatoes, seeded and chopped	

Sauté onions and peppers in hot bacon drippings over medium-high heat until they are tender, approximately 5 minutes. Add garlic and stir constantly to prevent scorching. Stir in tomatoes and remaining ingredients. Reduce heat and cook, stirring often, 10 minutes or until okra are tender.

6 to 8 servings

HOWARD HISTORY MAKER: Alexander T. Augusta was born free in Norfolk, Virginia, in 1825. He was covertly taught to read and write by an Episcopal bishop because at that time teaching blacks to read was illegal. Trained as a barber, Augustus went to California during the gold rush to earn money to pay for an academic education. Refused admission to U.S. medical schools, Augustus went north and received a medical degree from Trinity Medical College at the University of Toronto. In 1863 he was commissioned a major in the U.S. Army as a surgeon in the 7th U.S. Colored Troops, directly by the "hand of Abraham Lincoln," so becoming the first black surgeon and the first black major in the Union Army. Although he was one of only a few blacks to achieve field grade rank, he was paid black-enlisted wages for most of his tour of duty.

At the end of the Civil War, Augusta was brevetted Lt. Colonel, the first black officer granted this honor, making him the highest ranking black officer in the United States Army. In 1868, he became the first black to join the medical department faculty at Howard University, where he taught anatomy from 1868 to 1876.

COLLARD GREENS AND OKRA

Collard greens are a classic southern favorite, which I cannot imagine serving without homemade potato salad or candied yams. For the best flavor, avoid purchasing greens that are yellow, limp, or that have signs of wormholes. To best preserve their flavor after purchase, store greens by first wrapping them in damp paper towels. Next, place them in a plastic bag and refrigerate up to 3 days before preparing.

1 large ham hock	1 fresh jalapeño, seeded and chopped
4 bunches collard greens	2½ cups chopped ham
½ teaspoon salt	14–16 small okra pods
½ teaspoon sugar	

In a large pot combine ham hock with sufficient water to cover and bring to a rapid boil; reduce heat to medium, cover, and simmer 1 hour. While meat is simmering, clean greens by first removing and discarding any wilted, blemished, or yellow greens. After sorting greens in this manner, remove and discard coarse stems and leaf midribs. Next, fill sink with cold water and wash greens by plunging them up and down in the water. Depending on the sandiness of your greens, you may need to repeat this process several times. Stack 8 to 10 leaves at a time into a pile; roll cigar fashion and slice into ¼-inch strips. Transfer the greens to the pot containing cooked ham hock. Cover the pot and allow greens to simmer over medium heat for 45 minutes. Add salt, sugar, jalapeño pepper, and ham to greens and cook 20 minutes. While greens are cooking, wash okra and then cut off and discard stems. Layer okra on top of greens, cover the pot, and cook an additional 20 minutes or until okra are tender. Add water as necessary to prevent the greens from scorching.

6 servings

HOWARD HISTORY MAKER: An African-American surgical pioneer and innovator, Dr. Daniel Hale Williams performed the first open-heart surgery on a stabbing victim in 1893. He was appointed surgeon-in-chief of Freedmen's Hospital in 1894. He established a school of nursing, appointed the first interns, acquired the hospital's first ambulance, and was instrumental in reducing the hospital's mortality rate. He is often credited with (directly or indirectly) training most of the physicians of his generation. In 1913 Dr. Williams was the first African-American inducted into the American College of Surgeons as a charter fellow.

COLLARD GREENS AND SMOKED NECKBONES

1	pound pork neckbones		1	tablespoon bacon drippings
2	bunches collard greens— tender		¼	teaspoon crushed red pepper
				Salt and pepper to taste

Wash neckbones and place in a large pot with sufficient water to cover. Bring to a quick boil, reduce heat to medium-high, and simmer briskly for 1 to 1½ hours or until the meat is fork tender and just begins to fall from the bone.

While neckbones are simmering, clean greens by first removing and discarding any wilted, blemished, or yellow greens. After sorting greens in this manner, remove and discard coarse stems and leaf midribs. Next, fill sink with cold water and wash greens by plunging them up and down in the water. Depending on the sandiness of your greens, you may need to repeat this process several times. Stack 8 to 10 leaves at a time into a pile, roll cigar fashion, and slice into ¼-inch strips.

Remove the neckbones from the broth to a plate and set them aside to cool. If necessary, add additional water to the pot to equal 6 cups. Transfer the greens to the pot containing the broth. Cover the pot and allow greens to simmer over medium heat for 45 to 60 minutes. Return the neckbones to the pot, and add bacon drippings and crushed red pepper. Season the greens with salt and pepper to taste and mix well.

4 to 6 servings

HOWARD HISTORY NOTE: Founded in 1867, Howard University continues to attract the nation's top students and produces more on-campus African-American Ph.D.s than any other university in the world. So far the university has produced two Rhodes scholars, a Truman scholar, six Fulbright scholars, thirteen Pickering scholars, one Beinecke scholar, and two White House fellows.

TURNIP GREENS AND TURNIPS

Turnips are a wonderful root vegetable because they are rich in both flavor and vitamins. When selecting them, look for a smooth surface, approximately 2 to 3 inches across, and allow approximately ½ pound of turnip greens and turnips per guest.

1	large ham hock	¾	teaspoon salt
3	pounds turnip greens and turnips	1¼	teaspoon pepper

In a large pot, combine ham hock with sufficient water to cover and bring to a rapid boil; reduce heat to medium, cover, and simmer 1 hour. While meat is simmering, clean greens by first removing and discarding any wilted, blemished, or yellow greens. After sorting greens in this manner, remove and discard coarse stems and leaf midribs. Next, fill sink with cold water and wash greens by plunging them up and down in the water. Depending on the sandiness of your greens, you may need to repeat this process several times. Transfer the greens to the pot containing cooked ham hock. Trim and discard any stems or root ends from turnips. Scrub and quarter turnips, then place them in the pot on top of the greens. Cover and simmer over medium heat until greens are done and the turnips are fork tender, approximately 45 minutes to 1 hour. If necessary, cut greens up in the pot.

6 servings

SPINACH AND BACON

3	slices bacon	1	teaspoon salt
3	tablespoons onion, finely chopped	2	tablespoons water
2	pounds spinach (cleaned with long stems removed)	1	boiled egg, chopped coarsely

In a large pot, fry bacon until crisp and remove to a paper towel–lined plate to drain. Add onion and sauté until transparent. Add spinach, salt, and water. Cover the pot and continue to steam over medium heat for 3 to 5 minutes or until spinach is wilted and bright green, or continue to cook according to taste. Garnish with crumbled bacon and chopped boiled egg just before serving.

4 servings

SMOTHERED CABBAGE

My grandmother made the very best smothered cabbage, and I always loved smelling it cooking when I came in from play during one of my many summer visits. Usually, my grandmother would stand on the front porch, toss her head back, and call for us, enunciating each syllable of our names in perfect pitch, "CA-ROOOOOOO-LYYYYYYYNNNE, VIC-TOR-RI-AAAAH . . ." On cabbage day, she didn't have to call twice.

1	small, firm head of cabbage (1 to 1½-pounds)	¼	pound salt pork, diced
1	large onion, sliced thin	1	teaspoon salt
		¼	teaspoon black pepper

Wash and shred the cabbage into ½-inch strips. Place the cabbage and sliced onions into a colander, rinse under cold running water, and set aside to drain. While cabbage is draining, place salt pork in a heavy casserole and brown. When pork is brown, drain away all but 1 tablespoon of fat, leaving browned cubes in the pot. Add the cabbage and onion; stir well to coat. Add salt and pepper, cover tightly, and cook over medium heat for 20 minutes or until cabbage reaches the desired degree of tenderness.

4 servings

Dr. Charles Drew, originator of the blood bank and first African-American
to receive the doctor of science degree in medicine
(Photograph courtesy Howard University Archives)

Dr. Charles Drew

Charles Drew, born June 3, 1904, to Richard and Nora Drew, attended Dunbar High School in Washington, D.C., where he received the James E. Walker Memorial Medal for all-around athletic performance. At Amherst College, he was a star quarterback, the most valuable baseball player, captain of the track team, and national high hurdles champion, earning the Howard Hill Messman Trophy for his splendid athletic contribution there.

For two years after graduation, Drew was athletic director, football coach, and science instructor at Morgan State College in Baltimore. In 1928, he entered medical school at McGill University in Montreal, Canada, where Dr. John Beattie, a British professor, interested him in blood research. Finishing second in a class of 127, Drew graduated in

1933 as a member of Alpha Omega Alpha, the school's Medical Honorary Society, with master of surgery and doctor of medicine degrees. Drew continued to pursue his interest in blood research during his two year internship and residency at Montreal General Hospital and the Royal Victoria Hospital. In 1935 he returned to the United States, where he worked as a pathology instructor at Howard University and as a resident assistant in surgery at Freedmen's Hospital.

In 1938, he was awarded the Rockefeller Foundation Research Fellowship and spent two years in New York City, as a resident at the Columbia University Presbyterian Hospital. While studying methods of collection and long-term storage of blood needed for transfusions, his experiments led to the discovery that by separating plasma from whole blood and then refrigerating each separately, they could be combined up to a week later for a blood transfusion. Prior to his discoveries, blood could not be stored for more than two days because of the rapid breakdown of red blood cells. He also experimented with plasma, discovering that it could be used in place of whole blood, lasted longer, and was less likely to become contaminated. In addition, Drew discovered that while everyone has a specific blood type (A, B, AB, or O) which makes cross-type transfusion largely incompatible, everyone has the same type of plasma, and under certain circumstances plasma can be substituted for a whole-blood transfusion.

In 1940, when Dr. Drew earned his doctor of medical science degree from Columbia University, America was facing war. One problem confronting medical scientists was how to get life-saving blood to the front. Dr. Drew received a cablegram from his former professor, Dr. John Beattie, who had returned to England, urgently requesting 5,000 ampules of dried plasma for transfusions. Drew organized a blood bank in London during World War II and as medical supervisor of the "Blood for Britain" project, Dr. Drew helped save the lives of many wounded soldiers. Appointed the first medical director of the first American Red Cross Blood Bank in the United States in 1941, he resigned after the United States War Department issued a directive that blood taken from white donors should be segregated from that of black donors.

In 1942, Dr. Drew returned to Howard University to head its Department of Surgery and to serve as chief of surgery at Freedmen's Hospital, where in 1944 he was named chief of staff and medical director. In 1948 he was awarded the Spingarn Medal from the National Association for the Advancement of Colored People for his work on blood plasma. Among many other professional honors, he received the E. S. Jones Award for Research in Medical Science and became the first black to be appointed an examiner by the American Board of Surgery.

YELLOW SQUASH AND ONIONS

2   tablespoons bacon drippings
2   pounds yellow squash,
        scrubbed and sliced to a
        thickness of ½ inch
3   medium-size onions, peeled
        and sliced thin

1   small clove garlic, minced
1   teaspoon salt
¼   teaspoon pepper

Heat the bacon drippings over medium-high heat for approximately 2 minutes. Add remaining ingredients and stir gently to mix. Cover and cook over medium-low heat for 25 to 30 minutes or until squash is fork tender.

4 servings

BAKED TOMATOES

Tomatoes aren't just for salads and sauces anymore. They are excellent when baked and served as a side dish!

12 large tomatoes, peeled and
        sliced ¼-inch thick
    Salt and pepper
½   cup butter
2   cups bread crumbs

1½ teaspoons sugar
2   tablespoons minced parsley
    Butter
    Dry bread crumbs

Place a layer of tomatoes in a glass baking dish and salt and pepper them to taste. Rub the butter into the bread crumbs, and mix in sugar and parsley. Spread the mixture thickly on the tomatoes, using all of it, and add another layer of tomatoes. Dot with butter, sprinkle with dry bread crumbs, and bake 20 to 30 minutes or until the topping is golden brown.

2 to 4 servings

BAKED CORN

This simple dish is a family favorite that I remember my great-grandmother serving.

9	cups fresh corn, divided	¼	cup butter
½	cup heavy cream	2	tablespoons sugar
½	cup half-and-half		Pinch of nutmeg

Preheat oven to 325°F. Process or blend half the corn until it is creamy. Combine the creamed corn with the remaining ingredients in a large baking pan. Cover the pan with foil and bake 1½ hours, stirring frequently.

6 to 8 servings

Lab at Howard University, c.1900
(Corbis)

HOWARD UNIVERSITY HISTORY MAKER: A founder of Howard University Medical School, from 1868 to 1876 Dr. Charles B. Purvis was a member of the Medical Department, where he taught Materia Medica and Therapeutics, "Botany," and Materia Medica and Medical Jurisprudence, in addition to other subjects. Following the shooting of President James Garfield in 1881, Dr. Purvis, who was present at the time, attended to the president in an unsuccessful attempt to save his life.

ZESTY GRILLED CORN ON THE COB

Add a little spice to liven up your grilled corn and they will definitely come running back for more.

6 ears of corn on the cob with husks intact	¼ teaspoon coarsely ground pepper
¼ cup softened butter	¼ teaspoon cumin
¾ teaspoon salt	1½ teaspoons chili powder
	⅛ teaspoon ground nutmeg

Clean the corn by pulling husks down toward the bottom of the ear. Leave husks intact and remove silk from the corn. Combine remaining ingredients and generously butter each cob of corn. Return husks to original position and twist ends together. Adjust grill rack approximately 4 inches from hot coals. Grill, turning occasionally, until the corn is tender, approximately 15 to 20 minutes.

6 servings

FRESH GREEN PEAS AND DUMPLINGS

Garden-fresh peas herald the arrival of spring! Enjoy them as you remember your grandmother's front porch and the pea-shelling parties of your youth.

2 cups water	¾ cup whipping cream
3 pounds fresh, shelled, sweet green peas	2 tablespoons butter
3 fresh mint leaves	½ teaspoon salt

Prepare dumpling mix (recipe follows) and set aside. Bring water to a boil. Add peas and mint leaves. Drop dumplings from a teaspoon into the boiling peas, cover, and simmer 15 minutes, without disturbing. Drain, stir in whipping cream and remaining ingredients.

6 servings

DUMPLINGS

1 cup sifted flour	½ teaspoon salt
2 teaspoons sugar	1 tablespoon butter
1½ teaspoons baking powder	½ cup + 1 tablespoon half-and-half

In a small bowl, sift together flour, sugar, baking powder, and salt. Cut in the butter until the mixture resembles coarse corn meal. Add half-and-half and stir with a fork until the mixture is just combined.

4 to 6 servings

GREEN PEAS WITH MINT AND LEMON

3 pounds fresh shelled sweet green peas	3 tablespoons butter
1½ cups boiling water	2 teaspoons fresh mint, minced
1 teaspoon sugar	1 tablespoon lemon zest

Place peas in a saucepan and add boiling water and sugar. Cover saucepan and bring peas to a boil. Continue cooking until the peas are tender, approximately 8 to 10 minutes. Drain peas, add remaining ingredients, and toss lightly to mix.

6 servings

WHIPPED CARROTS

Carrots are a wonderful addition to your favorite meal because they add color, texture, and flavor. They contain natural sugar, and as a result, they do not require much additional sugar or preparation. To store carrots, first remove any green tops, which will dry out the root if left intact. Next, place them in the crisper and keep them cold and humid.

1 pound fresh carrots	¼ teaspoon ground ginger
¾ cup orange juice	1 teaspoon sugar
½ teaspoon salt	2 tablespoons butter
⅛ teaspoon ground nutmeg	2 tablespoons heavy cream

Scrub, rinse, and grate carrots. Combine with orange juice and bring to a boil; reduce heat, cover, and simmer 15 to 20 minutes, or until carrots are tender. Drain, mash, and add remaining ingredients. Whip lightly before serving.

4 to 6 servings

BRANDIED CARROTS

1	pound fresh carrots		1	teaspoon sugar
1	cup boiling water		3	tablespoons brandy
2	teaspoons butter			

Scrub carrots, rinse, and drain. Slice carrots into ½-inch pieces. Combine carrots and boiling water, place over medium heat and simmer, uncovered, until carrots reach the desired degree of tenderness. Drain carrots; add butter, sugar, and brandy. Heat through over low heat while stirring to prevent scorching.

4 servings

ROSEMARY AND THYME-SCENTED GREEN BEANS

1	pound fresh green beans, trimmed		1	tablespoon fresh thyme, chopped
1	tablespoon butter		¼	teaspoon fresh rosemary leaves (no stems)
1	tablespoon green pepper, chopped		1½	cups chicken broth + 1 chicken bouillon cube
1	clove garlic, minced			

Wash green beans and set aside to drain. Melt butter in a large saucepan over medium heat. Stir in green pepper and garlic; sauté for 2 to 3 minutes or until green peppers are soft. Add beans and remaining ingredients. Bring beans to a boil, reduce heat, cover, and simmer 10 minutes or until beans reach the desired degree of tenderness.

4 to 6 servings

GREEN BEANS AND MUSHROOMS

1½	pounds fresh green beans, trimmed	⅔	cup chicken broth
3	tablespoons butter	1	teaspoon salt
⅔	cup onion, finely chopped	¼	teaspoon + an additional pinch nutmeg
½	pound sliced mushrooms		

Wash green beans and set aside to drain. Melt butter in a large saucepan over medium heat. Stir in onion; sauté for 2 to 3 minutes or until onions are soft. Add mushrooms, sauté an additional 2 minutes. Add beans and remaining ingredients. Bring beans to a boil, reduce heat, cover, and simmer 10 minutes or until beans reach the desired degree of tenderness.

4 to 6 servings

BAKED ACORN SQUASH

1	large acorn squash	½	teaspoon pepper
4	tablespoons butter, melted	⅛	teaspoon onion powder
¾	teaspoon salt	⅛	teaspoon grated nutmeg

Preheat oven to 375°F. Quarter acorn squash and remove seeds and fiber with a spoon. Brush both sides of each squash quarter with butter and place in a large baking dish. Next, combine the remaining ingredients, mix well to blend, and use mixture to season squash to taste. Cover dish with foil and bake 45 minutes to 1 hour or until the squash flesh is fork tender. Remove from oven and, when squash is sufficiently cool to handle, remove the flesh from the rind, coarsely chop, and serve.

2 to 4 servings

SIDE DISHES

Howard University:
A Renaissance of Friends and Family

By the 1920s, Howard University was enjoying its well-earned reputation as a "Black Intellectual Mecca." Its faculty consisted of distinguished professors such as Rhodes Scholar Alain Locke and the pioneering civil rights lawyer Charles Hamilton Houston. The school's growing profile attracted other "notables" and "greats," such as President John F. Kennedy, President Lyndon Baines Johnson, Emperor Haile Selassie of Ethiopia, Mary McLeod Bethune, Hattie McDaniel and Duke Ellington. Some good friends who came to visit liked what they saw and stayed to join the "Howard Family." In the decades that followed Howard's influence was felt throughout the nation, but especially in our nation's capital. The focus on academics and achievement attracted some of the greatest men and women of the day, people whose names are now etched in history.

COUNTRY-STYLE BUTTER BEANS

1	pound butter beans		1	teaspoon salt
5	cups chicken broth		⅛	teaspoon pepper
3	tablespoons butter		½	cup heavy cream

Place the beans in a large colander and pick over to remove stones or other foreign objects. Rinse the beans in cold water, drain, and place them in a large bowl. Add sufficient water to cover by 3 inches. Soak overnight. Drain and rinse beans before cooking them. Cook lima beans in chicken broth until tender, 2½ to 3 hours. Drain and add butter, salt, pepper and heavy cream. Heat through before serving.

4 servings

BUTTER BEANS, BACON, AND TOMATOES

As children, my brother and I could never have enough of these beans, and sometimes we would compete for the last bowl!

5	slices bacon		4½	cups unsalted chicken broth
1	large onion		4½	cups fresh or frozen butter beans, thawed
1	medium green bell pepper, chopped		1	teaspoon salt
3	large cloves garlic		1	teaspoon pepper
3	medium-size tomatoes, peeled, seeded, and chopped		½	teaspoon Tabasco sauce

Fry bacon until crisp, remove to a paper towel–lined plate to drain, and reserve drippings. Stir in onion and next two ingredients and sauté until tender. Stir in tomatoes and cook an additional 3 minutes. Stir in the broth and butter beans and bring to a boil. Cover the pot and reduce heat to a simmer, stirring occasionally; cook 35 minutes. Add remaining ingredients, uncover, and continue to cook an additional 20 minutes.

6 to 8 servings

CHILI PINTO BEANS

4 slices bacon	¼ teaspoon salt,
1 large green pepper, chopped	2 cups tomatoes, diced
1 medium onion, chopped	1 tablespoon chili powder
3 cloves garlic, minced	Pinch of cumin
3 cups cooked pinto beans	Chopped jalapeño peppers for
1 teaspoon salt	garnish

Fry bacon until crisp, remove to a paper towel–lined plate to drain, and reserve drippings. Stir in green pepper and onion; sauté until onion is tender. Add garlic; stir and cook an additional 3 minutes. Crumble bacon; add bacon and remaining ingredients to bean pot and simmer for 45 minutes. Garnish with jalapeños to add more spice.

6 servings

BLACK-EYED PEAS WITH HAM AND TOMATOES

1	pound black-eyed peas	8	cups unsalted chicken broth, divided
5	slices bacon	1	tablespoon salt
1	cup chopped onion	1	teaspoon dried thyme
¼	cup chopped green pepper	⅛	teaspoon ground cayenne pepper
1	clove garlic, minced	2	tomatoes, peeled, seeded, and coarsely chopped
¼	cup celery, chopped		
2	cups cubed ham		

Place the peas in a large colander and pick over to remove stones or other foreign objects. Rinse the peas in cold water, drain, and place them in a large bowl. Add sufficient water to cover by 3 inches. Soak overnight. Drain. Place bacon in an 8-quart pot and cook until crisp; remove bacon to a paper towel–lined plate to drain, and reserve the drippings. Add onion, green pepper, garlic, and celery to bacon drippings and cook over medium-high heat until vegetables are tender. Add ham, cover with 5 cups chicken broth, 1 tablespoon of salt and thyme and bring to a rapid boil. Reduce heat, cover, and simmer for 1 hour. Add drained beans to the pot, cover and simmer 1 hour or until the beans are tender. Add additional broth or water as necessary to prevent the peas from sticking. Add remaining ingredients. Simmer uncovered for 30 minutes to allow the peas to cook down.

6 to 8 servings

OKRA FRITTERS

2	pounds fresh baby okra	¾	teaspoon salt
1	cup all-purpose flour	1	teaspoon black pepper
1	cup beer		Vegetable oil for frying

Steam okra until almost tender, approximately 3 minutes. Pat okra dry and allow to cool while whisking together the flour, beer, salt, and pepper. Place 2 to 3 inches of vegetable oil in a cast-iron skillet and heat to 375°. Dip okra in beer batter, allowing excess to drip off, and deep fry until golden brown, approximately 3 to 5 minutes.

4 servings

CORN FRITTERS

3 cups fresh corn cut from the cob	⅛ teaspoon nutmeg
¼ cup evaporated milk	Pinch of cayenne pepper
⅓ cup flour	1 egg, beaten
¼ cup corn meal	Vegetable oil
½ teaspoon salt	Chopped parsley

Combine corn, evaporated milk, flour, corn meal, salt, nutmeg, cayenne pepper, and egg. Place 2 inches of vegetable oil in a large skillet. Heat vegetable oil until a drop of batter placed in it sputters and drop corn patties by heaping teaspoonfuls into the hot oil. Fry until golden brown. Garnish with chopped parsley.

8 servings

BLACK-EYED PEA PATTIES

2 cups cooked black-eyed peas, mashed	Pinch of cayenne pepper
¼ cup flour	1½ cups corn meal
1 egg, beaten	1 teaspoon sugar
½ teaspoon salt	½ teaspoon salt
2 teaspoons onion, minced	White pepper to taste
	Vegetable oil for frying

Combine mashed peas, flour, egg, salt, onion, and cayenne pepper; mix well to blend and shape into 4 large or 6 small patties and set aside. In a separate bowl, combine the remaining ingredients except oil and mix well. Coat the patties in the corn meal mixture and place on a wax paper–lined tray, and refrigerate 1 hour to chill. Place 2 inches of vegetable oil in a large skillet. Heat vegetable oil just until a drop of water placed in it sputters, dust patties with a second coat of cornmeal, and place them carefully into the hot oil. Turn once when edges start to brown and continue to fry until golden.

4 to 6 servings

AKA Ivy Leaf Club at Howard University
(Photo courtesy Howard University Archives)

FRIED EGGPLANT

1	large eggplant	
¼	cup vegetable oil	
½	cup flour	
½	teaspoon salt	
⅛	teaspoon nutmeg	

Pinch of cayenne pepper
¾ cup milk, divided
1   egg, well beaten
Flour
Vegetable oil for frying

Peel eggplant, cube it into 1-inch squares, and soak in salted water for approximately 1 hour. While eggplant is soaking, place all of the remaining ingredients—except ¼ cup of the milk—in screw-top jar and shake until well blended. Add remaining milk, shake again, and set milk batter aside.

Drain eggplant and pat dry. Place eggplant in a bag of flour and shake to thoroughly coat. Dip in milk batter and deep fry in an inch of oil until golden brown. Avoid crowding the pan. Drain excess oil from the eggplant by setting it on paper towels for a moment or two before serving.

2 to 4 servings

FRENCH-FRIED ONION RINGS AND GREEN PEPPERS

	Vegetable oil	
2	large sweet onions, sliced into ½-inch rings	
1	large green bell pepper, seeded and sliced into ½-inch rings	
1¼	cups buttermilk	

1½ cups self-rising flour
1   teaspoon salt
¼   teaspoon onion powder
⅛   teaspoon garlic powder
¼   teaspoon white pepper
Vegetable oil for deep frying

Place onion and green pepper slices in a shallow nonreactive bowl and cover with buttermilk. Refrigerate for 1 hour. Combine flour, salt, onion powder, garlic powder, and white pepper in a large bowl and mix well. Remove onions and peppers from buttermilk bath, reserving buttermilk, and drain well. Toss onions and peppers with flour mixture, transfer to a colander, and shake excess flour from onions and peppers back into the bowl. Return onions and peppers to the buttermilk bath, drain, and flour again. Heat 3 to 4 inches of oil to frying temperature and cook in four batches until golden, approximately 3 minutes per batch. May also be cooked in a deep fryer according to manufacturer's directions. Drain on paper towels and keep in a warm oven. Sprinkle with salt just prior to serving with grilled T-bone steaks. See the recipe on page 203.

4 to 6 servings

BAKED CORN

4	slices of bacon	1	cup evaporated milk
¼	cup onion, chopped	1	egg, well beaten
¼	cup green pepper, chopped	1	teaspoon granulated sugar
¼	cup red pepper, chopped		Salt and pepper to taste
1	clove garlic, finely minced	1	tablespoon flour
1	16-ounce package frozen corn, thawed and drained		

Preheat oven to 350°F and lightly butter a 2-quart baking dish. In a large frying pan, fry bacon until crisp. Remove from pan and set aside on a paper towel–lined plate to drain. Add onion, green pepper, red pepper, and garlic to the pan and sauté until the onion is tender. Add corn and continue to cook and stir for 2 to 3 minutes. Add flour and crumbled bacon and stir until well blended. Remove the pan from the heat, add remaining ingredients and mix well before transferring to the prepared baking dish. Bake for 1 hour or until set and golden.

4 servings

A reception for Marion Anderson

The great contralto is well remembered for the concert she gave at the Lincoln Memorial on Easter Sunday, 1939, after she was denied the use of Constitutional Hall. Appalled at the denial, Eleanor Roosevelt, who had worked with a committee from Howard to bring Anderson to Washington, opened the Lincoln Memorial for the concert. Seventy-five thousand onlookers of all races listened as Miss Anderson sang "Nobody Knows the Trouble I've Seen" and "America." Among the guests greeting Miss Anderson is Dr. Mordecai Wyatt Johnson, son of a former slave and first African-American president of Howard University.

THREE-CHEESE MACARONI AND CHEESE

2	tablespoons butter, divided	⅛	teaspoon ground cayenne pepper
¼	cup all-purpose flour	¼	cup shredded Cheddar cheese
1	quart milk	¾	cup shredded Fontina cheese
1	teaspoon dry mustard	¼	cup freshly grated Parmesan cheese
¾	teaspoon salt	1½	cups fresh bread crumbs
¼	teaspoon ground white pepper	1	tablespoon chopped fresh parsley

Preheat oven to 375°F. Melt 1 tablespoon butter in a large saucepan over medium-high heat. Whisk flour into the butter and continue to cook and whisk for 1 minute. Gradually whisk in the milk, mustard, salt, and peppers. Bring to a boil while continuing to whisk. Allow mixture to boil for 1 minute before removing the pan from the heat and whisking in the three cheeses until the cheese melts.

Cook the macaroni according to package directions or just until tender, approximately 8 minutes. Drain macaroni and stir into the cheese sauce. Pour the mixture into a lightly buttered baking dish. Melt remaining butter and stir into bread crumbs. Add parsley and mix well before spreading over the macaroni. Bake in the preheated oven for approximately 30 minutes. Allow it to stand 5 minutes before serving.

4 to 6 servings

CORNBREAD, COUNTRY SAUSAGE, AND PECAN DRESSING

This dressing is not your typical Southern fare. It is more crumbly than what you may be used to. However, it always receives high marks when I serve it to family and friends.

1 pound ground pork sausage meat (Jimmy Dean Sage, for instance)
2 tablespoons butter
2¼ cups onion, finely chopped
1 cup celery, including some tops, finely chopped
½ cup green pepper, chopped
1 large clove garlic, minced
2 cups chicken broth

1 teaspoon salt (optional)
½ teaspoon coarsely ground pepper
1 teaspoon sage
4¼ cups crumbled cornbread (approximately 2 pans of J.R.'s Skillet Cornbread, page 236)
½ cup chopped hazelnuts, lightly toasted

Place sausage in a large skillet and cook over medium-high heat until pink disappears, but do not brown, approximately 10 minutes. Stir frequently to break up sausage until it resembles ground beef for chili or spaghetti. Use a slotted spoon to remove sausage from the skillet to a large bowl. Retain up to 1 tablespoon of the sausage drippings in the skillet. If necessary, add sufficient vegetable oil to equal 1 tablespoon. Add butter, onion, celery, pepper and garlic; cook, stirring occasionally, until vegetables are limp and transparent, 6 to 8 minutes. Stir in broth, salt, pepper, and sage; heat to boiling, stirring to loosen any sediment from the bottom of the skillet. Add broth mixture to the cornbread crumbs and hazelnuts; mix well. Use to stuff a young 10- to 14-pound turkey and cook according to packaging directions. Or, spoon dressing into a greased 2½-quart casserole. Bake in a 325°F oven for 1 hour.

8 to 10 servings

Baked Potato Notes: The secret ingredient is patience: Great baked potatoes require high temperatures and long baking time.

Anyone can make fabulous baked potatoes by simply adhering to a few rules of thumb: Always use the right potato for the job: a baking potato such as the Idaho Russet as opposed to a boiling potato such as Yukon Gold. This is one time that fresh is not always best. Some baked potato connoisseurs also suggest that a slightly older potato bakes better than a newer one and advise purchasing your potatoes a week in advance of cooking them. Select firm, unsprouted potatoes with no green on the skin and store them in a cool, dark, dry place. Exposure to light will discolor potatoes and refrigeration will alter their flavor.

The potato should not be wrapped in foil; wrapping traps the steam inside during cooking, which results in a less fluffy, steamed potato. Microwaving the potato produces similar dense results. Instead, use a table fork and pierce the entire surface of the potato to a ¼-inch depth before baking at 450°F. for 1¼ hours or until a skewer slides through with ease.

BAKED POTATOES

They won't leave one bite on their plates, not even the delicious skin!

4	baking potatoes	½	teaspoon coarsely grated black
1	teaspoon onion powder		pepper
2	tablespoons kosher salt		

Rinse baking potatoes and dry really well; rub the outside of each potato with oil and prick all over with a fork. Rub the potato with mixture of onion powder, salt, and coarsely grated black pepper. Bake at 450°F for 1¼ hours, or until the outside of the potato is crisp and the inside light and fluffy. Serve with butter, sour cream, and chives.

4 servings

BAKED POTATOES II

4	large baking potatoes	Kosher salt
2	tablespoons bacon drippings or vegetable oil	

Scrub potatoes, rinse, and drain well. Pierce each potato several times to allow steam to escape. Rub the outside of each potato with drippings or oil. Sprinkle the outside of each potato with kosher salt, place on a baking sheet, and bake in a preheated 400°F oven for 1½ to 2 hours or until the potatoes are fork tender. When the potatoes are done, cut an "X" into the top of each and squeeze gently. Dress with butter and salt and pepper.

4 servings

JOHN QUICK'S BETTER CHEDDAR CHEESE BAKED POTATOES

The experts will say that because these potatoes are wrapped in foil before baking, technically they are steamed potatoes. But I say who needs an expert to tell you when you're having a truly magnificent potato dining experience. This recipe is among my favorites.

4	slices of bacon		4	baking potatoes
2	tablespoons onion, finely chopped			Kosher salt and pepper to taste
2	tablespoons green pepper, finely chopped			Cheddar cheese

Fry bacon until crisp and remove to a paper towel–lined plate to drain. Remove all but 2 tablespoons of drippings from the pan and sauté onion and pepper. Wash potatoes under cold, running water, pat dry, and roll them in the salt. Butterfly the potatoes lengthwise (leaving the bottom skin intact). Fill each potato with the onion and pepper mixture, salt and pepper to taste. Close each potato and wrap in aluminum foil. Preheat the oven to 450° F. Place the wrapped potatoes on a baking sheet and bake until they are fork tender, approximately 1½ hours. At the end of cooking time, cut through the foil and push the potato ends toward each other while protecting fingers with a towel or oven mitts. Gently mash and fluff potatoes with a fork. Crumble reserved bacon and use to garnish potatoes, add cheese to taste, and return to oven to warm the potato through and melt cheese, approximately 5 to 7 minutes.

4 servings

STUFFED BAKED POTATOES

2	large baking potatoes	¼	cup heavy cream
2	tablespoons butter		Chopped chives
	Salt and white pepper to taste		

Preheat oven to 400°F. Pierce the potatoes to permit steam to escape. Bake potatoes for 45 to 60 minutes, or until potatoes are fork tender. When potatoes are done, cut off the top quarter lengthwise. Carefully remove the insides of the potatoes, keeping the shell intact. Mash the potatoes, add butter, and mix well until butter melts. Salt and pepper the potatoes to taste and stir in up to ¼ cup cream. Refill potato shells and garnish with chives.

4 servings

POTATOES AU GRATIN

The secret is in the green onion, which adds a little zest to this standard potato dish.

8	medium potatoes, baked, peeled, and sliced thin	2	tablespoons sour cream
¼	cup melted butter	1	cup table cream
3	tablespoons flour	1	cup milk
¼	teaspoon paprika	1½	cups grated sharp Cheddar cheese
¾	teaspoon salt	¼	cup green onions, including some tops for color, finely sliced
¼	teaspoon white pepper		Paprika

Preheat oven to 350°F. Lightly butter a glass or ceramic baking dish and evenly distribute the potatoes in the dish. Melt butter in a saucepan over medium-high heat, stir in flour until it is well blended. Add paprika, salt, pepper, sour cream, table cream, and milk; mix well. Bring mixture to a simmer, but do not boil. Allow mixture to simmer 3 to 4 minutes before pouring over the potatoes, sprinkle with cheese and onions, and mix to combine. Spoon mixture into a buttered casserole. Garnish with paprika and place potatoes in preheated oven and bake for 35 to 40 minutes or until the potatoes are golden.

4 servings

SCALLOPED POTATOES WITH HAM

	Butter	1¼	cup cubed, cooked ham
3	tablespoons butter	1	teaspoon salt
3	tablespoons flour	¼	teaspoon white pepper
2	cups milk	3	cups (¾ pound) shredded Cheddar cheese
4 or 5	large potatoes, peeled and sliced	⅓	cup grated Parmesan cheese
1	large onion, chopped	½	teaspoon ground paprika

Preheat oven to 350°F. Butter a 1- to 2-quart casserole. Melt 3 tablespoons butter in saucepan over low heat, add flour, and stir until smooth. Cook 1 minute while stirring constantly. Gradually stir in milk while cooking over medium heat until thickened.

Layer half the potato slices, onion, ham, salt, pepper, cheeses, and white sauce in order given. Repeat for second layer. Sprinkle with paprika and cover and bake at 350°F for 1 hour and 15 minutes.

4 to 6 servings

HOWARD HISTORY MAKER: Howard University professor and first African-American Rhodes Scholar Alain LeRoy Locke, a leader in the Harlem Renaissance movement, died in New York on June 10, 1954. Locke was influential in identifying, nurturing, and publishing the works of young, black artists such as former Howard student and Zeta Phi Beta soror Zora Neale Hurston.

CREAMED NEW POTATOES

High in fiber, potatoes are a significant source of vitamins C and B$_6$ and niacin, and as a result, are best eaten with the peel on.

1½	pounds small, new potatoes		½	teaspoon salt
1	tablespoon butter		3	tablespoons minced chives
1	cup sour cream			

Scrub and rinse the potatoes. Pare off a strip around the middle of each potato and boil in salted water for 20 minutes or until the potatoes are fork tender. Drain and add butter. Combine sour cream, salt, and chives. Pour over hot potatoes and heat through for an additional 2 to 3 minutes while gently tossing to ensure potatoes are evenly coated.

4 servings

ROASTED GARLIC MASHED POTATOES

They'll come running to the dinner table when they catch a whiff of the aroma of these appetizing potatoes.

2	pounds unpeeled red potatoes		2	heads (approximately 2 tablespoons) roasted garlic *(recipe follows on page 170)*
2	tablespoons butter			
2	tablespoons olive oil			Salt and pepper to taste
	Up to ⅔ cup half-and-half			

Preheat oven to 350°F. Place potatoes on a baking sheet in the oven and bake for 40 to 50 minutes or until the potatoes are very soft. At the end of cooking time, remove the potatoes from the oven and, when they are sufficiently cool to handle, remove the skin from approximately half of the potatoes. Combine the peeled and unpeeled potatoes and coarsely chop. Place them in a mixing bowl, add the butter and olive oil, and beat with an electric mixer, gradually adding the half-and-half until the potatoes reach the desired consistency. Add roasted garlic and salt and pepper to taste. Reheat the potatoes just prior to serving.

4 servings

HOWARD HISTORY MAKER: In 1960 James M. Nabrit, former dean of the Howard Law School, is named president of Howard University. A leading constitutional lawyer, Nabrit established the first systematic civil rights course at Howard, the first such course at an American law school.

ROASTED GARLIC

Roasting brings out a mellow nuttiness in garlic, which imparts a deliciously different flavor to a number of dishes.

2 medium heads of garlic	4 teaspoons olive oil, divided

Remove the dry outer layers of skin from the garlic heads. (Each medium-size head yields approximately 1 tablespoon of garlic paste.) However, leave the moist shiny skin encasing the whole bulb intact. Using a sharp knife, remove approximately 1/4 inch of the pointy top portion of the bulb of garlic, again leaving the bulb intact, but exposing the individual cloves of garlic. Place the bulbs cut side up in a small baking dish (specially designed covered ceramic dishes may be purchased at most cooking specialty shops) and drizzle them evenly with divided olive oil. Cover the baking dish and bake in preheated oven for 25 to 30 minutes or until cloves are very soft.

When bulbs are sufficiently cool to handle, squeeze the roasted garlic cloves out of their skin or remove the cloves with the tip of a small knife into a pestle or small bowl. Use a mortar or the back of a spoon to mash the cloves smooth. Use paste as desired.

It might be a good idea to roast several bulbs at a time to have the paste on hand for seasoning. Freeze the paste in ice cube trays or wrap small portions in heavy plastic wrap; put into freezer bags. Thaw to use. Or, refrigerate the paste in an airtight container or wrapped in heavy plastic for up to one week. The garlic paste is great all by itself as a butter-like spread on Cuban, French, or Italian bread or you can combine it with creamed cheese for a delicious spread. The next time you melt butter to serve with crab or lobster, add some of the roasted garlic as a scrumptious flavor enhancer.

ROASTED POTATOES WITH ONION AND ROASTED GARLIC

2	pounds red potatoes	2	tablespoons butter
2	pounds very small yellow onions	¼	cup heavy cream
1	tablespoon roasted garlic paste *(see recipe opposite)*		

Preheat oven to 400°F. Wash potatoes and prick all over with a fork. Place potatoes and onions with peels intact on a non-stick baking tray and roast in preheated oven for 45 minutes until fork tender. Check often and cook longer if necessary. While onions are cooling, use a mixer to mash the potatoes with their skin still intact. When the onions are sufficiently cool to handle, slip their skins off and puree. Add pureed onion, roasted garlic, butter, and cream to potato mixture and mix well to blend. Reheat if necessary.

8 servings

MUSHROOM AND RICE PILAF

3	tablespoons butter	2	cups rice cooked according to package directions (substitute chicken broth for water)
1	cup mushrooms, sliced	½	cup pine nuts
½	cup celery, coarsely chopped		
½	cup green onions, including some tops, sliced thin		

Melt butter in a large skillet over medium-high heat. Add mushrooms, celery, and green onions, and stir and cook until vegetables are tender. Add cooked rice, stir and cook until rice is warmed through. Add the pine nuts and serve immediately.

4 servings

Freedom is the right to share, share fully and equally, in American society—to vote, to hold a job, to enter a public place, to go to school. It is the right to be treated in every part of our national life as a person equal in dignity and promise to all others.

—President Lyndon Johnson's commencement address at Howard University,
"To Fulfill These Rights," June 4, 1965

Howard president James Nabrit, Jr., is seen adjusting the hood of U.S. president
Lyndon Baines Johnson as Johnson prepares to receive an honorary doctorate at Howard University.

BACON, OKRA, HAM, AND TOMATO RICE

5	slices bacon, chopped	2	cloves of garlic, minced
1	large onion, chopped	1¼	cups ham, chopped
1	small green bell pepper, chopped	1	14-ounce can diced tomatoes, drained
1	teaspoon jalapeño pepper, seeded and chopped	1	teaspoon dried thyme
1	cup okra, thinly sliced	1	cup uncooked long-grain rice
		2	cups unsalted chicken broth

Render bacon in a Dutch oven until browned, but not crisp. Stir in onion, green bell pepper, jalapeño pepper, and okra; sauté until the onion is tender. Add garlic and ham; continue cooking for 5 minutes. Add tomatoes, thyme, rice, and chicken broth. Bring mixture to a boil over high heat, cover, and simmer for approximately 30 minutes or until the rice is tender.

4 to 6 servings

FRIED APPLES

3	large tart apples, pared, cored, and cut into 8 wedges	1½	teaspoons ground cinnamon
		⅛	teaspoon ground allspice
3	tablespoons flour	2	tablespoons butter
½	cup sugar	¼	cup water

Rinse apples with cold running water and place in a colander to drain. Combine flour, sugar, cinnamon, and allspice; mix well to blend. Place sugar mixture and apples in a paper bag and shake to coat. Melt butter in a large frying pan over medium-high heat. Fry apples for 5 to 7 minutes, stirring often to prevent burning. Add water, reduce heat to medium low, and simmer for an additional 5 minutes. Check often and add additional water as necessary to prevent scorching.

4 to 6 servings

MAIN DISHES

Seen here *(standing, third from right)* at a Rhodes Scholar dinner, Alain Locke was the first African-American Rhodes Scholar. A member Phi Beta Sigma, founded at Howard University January 9, 1914, he became a chief interpreter and leader of the Harlem Renaissance movement.

Alain Le Roy Locke

The Younger Generation comes, bringing its gifts. They are the first fruits of the Negro Renaissance. Youth speaks, and the voice of the New Negro is heard.

—Alain Locke,
"Negro Youth Speaks," 1925

Not only an intellectual Mecca, Howard University was also a well-regarded fine arts center. During the 1920s, the Harlem Renaissance, a creative rebirth of African-American arts, was taking place in uptown New York and spreading across the nation. At the heart of this national cultural movement, sometimes referred to as the era of the "New Negro," was a Howard professor often considered the architect of the movement, Dr. Alain Locke.

Alain Le Roy Locke was born to Pliny Ishmael Locke and Mary Hawkins Locke in Philadelphia on September 13, 1886. A gifted student, Locke entered Harvard College in 1904, where he studied philosophy under celebrated faculty members Josiah Royce, Hugo Munsterberg, and George Santayana. Locke thrived in the competitive academic environment, was elected Phi Beta Kappa, and became the first African-American Rhodes Scholar. He studied at Hertford College, Oxford University, from 1907 to 1910, and at the University of Berlin for the academic year 1910 to 1911. He received his Ph.D. from Harvard in 1918. While completing requirements for his Ph.D., Locke had joined the Howard faculty in 1912, where he taught until his retirement in 1953 as head of the Department of Philosophy.

In 1923, Locke, already gaining prominence as a black intellectual, was invited to edit a special issue of the *Survey Graphic,* devoted entirely to the subject of race. He used the opportunity to showcase gifted African-American writers. Subtitled *Harlem: Mecca of the New Negro,* the March issue of the *Survey Graphic* featured the poetry, fiction, and essays of rising luminaries such as Howard University Trustee W.E.B. DuBois, James Weldon Johnson, Langston Hughes, Countee Cullen, Jean Toomer, and Anne Spencer.

The issue was so well received that within eight months it was expanded into a book. *The New Negro: An Interpretation,* published in 1925, is considered by some to be the definitive anthology of the Harlem Renaissance. The book featured additional Harlem Renaissance writers such as Zora Neale Hurston, a former Howard student whom Locke continued to mentor; Claude McKay; Angelina Grimke; and Jessie Fauset. Essays by academic intellectuals such as William Stanley Braithwaite, Howard professors Kelly Miller, J. A. Rogers, and Howard graduate E. Franklin Frazier were also included.

CRISPY FRIED CHICKEN

When I was a child, this chicken was a Saturday night favorite. After dinner, friends and I would use a little of the chicken grease and a slice of bread to polish our black patent leather shoes for church the following morning. Don't pretend you don't remember, Barbara Ann!

1	3-pound fryer chicken, cut up	1	teaspoon dried thyme
1	cup milk	½	teaspoon freshly ground pepper
2	teaspoons paprika	½	cup flour
1½	teaspoons salt	½	cup milk
1	teaspoon garlic powder		Vegetable shortening
		2	tablespoons bacon drippings

If cutting the chicken yourself, take care to keep skin intact. Wash chicken under running water and pat dry. Place in milk bath and refrigerate one hour before cooking. Turn chicken at the halfway point (½ hour). Combine next 5 ingredients, mix well, and use half of the mixture to season chicken. Place remaining seasoning and flour in a heavy paper bag and shake till well blended.

Place a large cast-iron skillet over moderate heat, fill to the halfway point with melted Crisco, and add the bacon grease. When a drop of water causes the shortening to sputter, remove chicken from refrigerator, turn chicken once more to coat with milk, and place pieces in the bag with seasoned flour. Shake vigorously to coat evenly. Shake excess flour back into the bag, and place chicken, without crowding, into pan. Fry until golden brown and crisp, 15 to 20 minutes before turning. (Turn only once during the cooking process.) Reduce heat to 350°F and fry till golden brown, approximately 15 additional minutes. Remove chicken to a paper bag or paper towel–lined plate and drain. Repeat the process until all chicken is fried, adding a little more shortening and bacon grease if necessary while maintaining a moderate fire beneath your pan.

Transfer the chicken to a large platter and do not cover. Serve warm or at room temperature.

8 servings

SPICY FRIED CHICKEN

1	3-pound fryer chicken, cut up	3	tablespoons flour
3	6-ounce packages powdered Italian salad dressing mix	2	teaspoons salt
¼	teaspoon onion powder	¼	cup fresh lemon juice
⅛	teaspoon garlic powder	1½	cups pancake flour
⅛	teaspoon cayenne pepper	2	tablespoons vegetable oil
			Club soda, chilled

Wash chicken under cold running water and set aside to drain. Combine the next seven ingredients. Spread mix evenly over each piece of chicken, cover with lemon juice, and refrigerate overnight. The next day, combine pancake flour with remaining powdered Italian salad dressing mix; blend well and set aside. Place approximately 1 inch of cooking oil in a cast iron skillet and heat to 400° to 425°F. While oil is heating pour club soda in a bowl of sufficient size to dip chicken into. Remove chicken from the refrigerator and quickly dip each piece of chicken in club soda, then dust it with the pancake flour mixture. Preheat oven to 400°F. Fry chicken for 5 minutes on each side to brown before placing it in preheated oven and baking for 30 to 35 minutes until the chicken is tender. During baking process, lightly mist chicken with water and sprinkle with pancake flour mixture.

4 to 6 servings

YOUR GRANDMOTHER'S ROASTED CHICKEN AND GRAVY

ROASTED CHICKEN

1	5-pound roasting hen	1	cup flour
¼	teaspoon celery seed	4	tablespoons butter
¼	teaspoon thyme	2	stalks celery, washed and cut in half
1	teaspoon pepper	3	small cloves garlic, peeled and crushed
¼	teaspoon cumin		
1	tablespoon dried rosemary, crushed	1	large onion, coarsely grated
1	tablespoon seasoned salt	1	large green pepper, seeded and quartered
2	teaspoons garlic powder	½	cup boiling chicken broth
1	teaspoon rubbed sage	¼	cup bacon drippings

Set oven rack one notch below the middle and preheat oven to 400°F. Remove giblets and neck from hen and set aside for use in making gravy. Wash hen, pat dry, and set aside. Combine next eight seasoning ingredients, mix well, and use to season hen, inside and out. Tie legs together and with breast side up, lift wings up toward the neck, and then fold wing tips beneath the back of the wings. Dredge the seasoned hen with flour and place it on its back in a dripping pan. Place butter, celery, garlic, onion, and green pepper inside the hen. Place hen, breast side up, in the preheated oven, and when flour is browned, after approximately 25 to 35 minutes, reduce heat to 350°F. Combine chicken broth and bacon drippings and baste every ½ hour. Cook an additional hour and fifteen minutes to an hour and a half or until vegetables are tender and juices run clear when the thickest part of the thigh is pierced with a fork. A meat thermometer inserted into thickest part of thigh next to body should register 175° to 180°F. Place on a warm serving platter and surround with vegetables.

4 to 6 servings

CHICKEN AND GIBLET GRAVY

Chicken giblets and neck
4   cups chicken broth plus
    additional for gravy
½   cup onion, chopped
¼   cup celery, chopped

1   bay leaf
    Pan drippings
⅓   cup flour
½   teaspoon salt
¼   cup half-and-half

In a 3-quart saucepan, combine giblets (do not add liver as it tends to make the gravy bitter), neck, broth, onion, celery, and bay leaf. Bring to a boil over high heat. Reduce heat to low and simmer 45 minutes. Strain giblets and neck from saucepan and set aside on a small saucer to cool. Remove and discard bay leaf. Pour giblets and broth into a bowl, cover, and set aside. While giblets are cooling, deglaze your roasting pan by adding 1 cup of the hot giblet broth to the pan. Place pan over medium-high heat, and boil 1 minute, stirring to loosen brown bits from the pan. Strain grease from drippings and reserve grease. Combine broth, pan drippings, and additional broth to equal 3 cups total. Spoon 3 tablespoons of the reserved grease back into the saucepan. Stir flour and salt into fat in the saucepan; cook over medium heat, stirring until flour turns golden. Gradually stir in broth mixture and cook, stirring until gravy boils and is slightly thickened. Remove meat from neck and discard neck bone. Coarsely chop neck meat and giblets and add to gravy. Stir in half-and-half.

6 servings

QUICK CHICKEN GRAVY

2   tablespoons butter
2   tablespoons all-purpose flour
1¼ cups chicken broth

½   cup half-and-half
    Salt and pepper to taste

In a large saucepan, over medium-high heat, melt butter, whisk in flour, and cook, while continuing to whisk for 1 minute. Add remaining ingredients, while continuing to whisk. Reduce heat to medium and continue to cook and whisk an additional 2 minutes, or until mixture reaches the desired consistency.

Yields 1½ cups

Soror Zora Neale Hurston
The renowned writer, anthropologist, and leading figure of the Harlem Renaissance
was a distinguished member of Zeta Phi Beta Sorority.

Zora Neale Hurston:
Daughter of the South, Literary Genius, Novelist, Folklorist, Anthropologist

Many years ago, Zora Neale Hurston wrote about what it was like for her to listen to Howard's alma mater being sung—on a day much like today. "My soul"— she said—"stood on tip toe and stretched up to take in all that it meant. So I was careful to do my class work and be worthy to stand there under the shadow of the hovering spirit of Howard. I felt the ladder beneath my feet."

—First Lady Hillary Clinton, quoting Hurston
at the 1998 Howard University commencement exercises

Much of Zora Neale Hurston's life is shrouded in mystery, and although the date and place of her birth have been debated, scholars now believe that she was born on January 7, 1891, in Notasulga, Alabama. During her early childhood, her family moved to an all-black town, Eatonville, Florida, which remained a strong influence in her life and writings. She glorified it as a place where African-Americans could be who they wanted to be, and in years to come, with her hat jauntily perched on her head and a cigarette carelessly dangling from her fingers, Hurston would regale Harlem society with tales of Eatonville, where her father, a carpenter and preacher, was several times elected mayor.

The fifth of eight children born to John Hurston and schoolteacher Lucy Ann Potts Hurston, thirteen-year-old Zora's life took a dramatic turn when her mother died. Following the remarriage of her father, Zora was "passed around the family like a bad penny" for the next several years. Frequent moves interrupted her education. As a young adult, supporting herself as a domestic in Baltimore, her employer assisted her in entering Morgan Academy, the high-school division of Morgan College (now Morgan State University). In 1920 she was accepted as a student at Howard University, where she studied on and off for four years while supporting herself as a manicurist. At Howard, she attracted the attention of philosophy professor Dr. Alain Locke, an authority on black culture. She also joined a literary club sponsored by Professor Locke and Montgomery Gregory, professor of English and drama, another key figure in the Harlem Renaissance.

The force from somewhere in Space which commands you to write in the first place, gives you no choice. You take up the pen when you are told, and write what is commanded. There is no agony like bearing an untold story inside you.

—Zora Neale Hurston

Hurston accepted a scholarship from Barnard College in New York City, where she studied anthropology and received her bachelor of arts in 1928. While studying under famed anthropologist Franz Boas, she received a fellowship from the Association of Negro Life and History and commenced field research in the South. Her results were published in the article "Cudjo's Own Story of the Last African Slaves," the source of which was later questioned. While in New York, she joined a collective of Harlem-based African-American musicians, artists, and writers, including Langston Hughes.

In 1930 she and Hughes collaborated on *Mule Bone: A Comedy of Negro Life.* Artistic differences arose that ended their friendship, and the play was not performed until its debut at New York's Lincoln Center Theater in 1991. Hurston's first novel, *Jonah's Gourd,* published in 1934, tells the story of a black Baptist preacher with a weakness for women. *Mules and Men,* an anthropologist's look at the folkways and songs of the rural South, followed in 1935. *Tell My Horse,* published in 1938, is a travelogue and study of Caribbean voodoo. Her second novel, *Their Eyes Were Watching God,* in which she tells the poignant story of a quadroon named Jessie, is her most critically acclaimed work.

Sterling A. Brown

Sterling Allen Brown was born on the campus of Howard University on May 1, 1901. He was the youngest son of Adelaide Allen and her husband, a former slave who pastored the Lincoln Temple Congregational Church and taught religion at Howard.

A champion of blues and jazz as legitimate art forms, he was elected to the Academy of American Poets and named poet laureate of the District of Columbia.

At Dunbar High School, he was taught by Haley Douglass, the grandson of abolitionist Frederick Douglass, and by Jessie Redmon Fauset, the novelist and a founding member of the National Association for the Advancement of Colored People. At home, where he was encouraged to read African-American literature, including works of Paul Laurence Dunbar, he met scholars and intellectual greats such as W.E.B. Du Bois and Alain

Professor Sterling A. Brown

Locke. In 1918, seventeen-year-old Brown accepted a scholarship to Williams College, where he began his lifelong love affair with jazz and blues, and graduated Phi Beta Kappa in 1922.

After earning a master's from Harvard University, Brown taught at a number of top-tier universities including Fisk and Howard, where he taught in the English Department for forty years. He mentored students such as civil rights activist Stokely Carmichael and actor Ossie Davis. His students lovingly nicknamed him the Red Ink Man, because of his famously numerous corrections to their class papers.

HERB CHICKEN AND VEGETABLES

1	3½-pound roasting chicken
1	tablespoon salt
2	teaspoons pepper
3	sprigs plus 1 tablespoon fresh rosemary, chopped
2	teaspoons fresh thyme, finely minced
2	teaspoons fresh basil, finely chopped
16	baby carrots
8	new potatoes, halved
4	stalks celery, including some leaves, sliced in 2-inch pieces
2	medium onions, cut into 1-inch wedges

Preheat oven to 375°F. Wash chicken under cold running water and pat dry. Combine salt and pepper and use to season chicken, inside and out, according to taste. Place rosemary, thyme, and basil in cavity. Truss legs and with breast side up, lift wings up toward the neck, and then fold wing tips beneath the back of the wings. Place chicken, breast side up, in a medium-size roasting pan. Place remaining ingredients around the chicken and bake 1½ to 1¾ hours or until vegetables are tender and juices run clear when the thickest part of the thigh is pierced with a fork. A meat thermometer inserted into the thickest part of thigh next to body should register 175 to 180°F. Do not allow thermometer to touch bone. Place on a warm serving platter and surround with vegetables.

6 servings

CHICKEN WINGS AND RICE

2	pounds chicken wings
1	tablespoon salt
¾	teaspoon paprika
¼	teaspoon chili powder
½	teaspoon cumin
¾	teaspoon ground black pepper
⅛	teaspoon cayenne pepper
¼	cup olive oil
1	large onion, chopped
1	large green bell pepper, seeded and chopped
3	garlic cloves, minced
1	cup uncooked long-grain rice
1	14½-ounce can chicken broth
1	14½-ounce can diced tomatoes, undrained

Wash wings under cold running water. Remove and discard wing tips. Combine next 6 seasoning ingredients and mix well. Use mixture to season the chicken to taste and set aside. Pour oil into a Dutch oven to a depth of 2 inches and heat to 375°F. Fry wings in batches, approximately 12 minutes, and set aside to drain. Add onion, bell pepper, and garlic and sauté for 5 minutes or until the vegetables are tender. Add rice and stir and sauté for 3 minutes until rice glistens. Add wings and remaining ingredients. Add 1½ teaspoons of the seasoning mix, cover, reduce heat, and simmer 40 minutes or until rice is tender. Add additional seasoning mix to taste.

6 servings

HOWARD HISTORY NOTE: Howard University professors Alain Locke and T. Montgomery Gregory published *Plays of Negro Life* in 1927.

Thomas Montgomery Gregory

After graduating from Harvard in 1910 with classmate T. S. Eliot, T. Montgomery Gregory joined the faculty at Howard University as an English instructor. There he founded the celebrated Howard Players, America's first black college theatre troupe.

Gregory's arrival was a homecoming; his childhood home had stood on the present site of Howard's Ira Aldridge Theatre. His father, James Monroe Gregory, had been the first student to enroll in the University's college department and was one of three men comprising the first graduating class. His mother, Fannie Emma Hagan, an advocate of women's issues and student mentor, was also a Howard alumna.

In 1919, Gregory was appointed the first director of the drama department, where he mentored young talents such as Helen Webb, May Miller, and writer/choreographer Ottie B. Graham, all of whom went on to establish successful careers in the theatre.

BBQ Chicken from a Southern Oven

1	young 3½-pound roasting chicken, split		1	teaspoon dry mustard
½	cup melted butter		1½	teaspoons Worcestershire sauce
¼	cup cider vinegar		⅛	teaspoon cayenne pepper

Preheat oven to 350°F. Wash chicken under cold running water, pat dry, and place skin side down in a shallow roasting pan on a rack. Combine remaining ingredients and set aside for basting. Cook for 1½ hours to 1¾ hours, basting every 15 minutes.

6 servings

Smothered Quail

½	cup all purpose flour		6	quail, dressed
1	teaspoon salt		½	cup vegetable oil
¾	teaspoon white pepper		2	cups chicken broth
⅛	teaspoon cayenne pepper			

Combine first 4 ingredients, mix well, and dredge quail in the mixture. Reserve remainder of flour mixture for future use. In a cast-iron skillet, heat vegetable oil until a drop of water placed in it sputters. Sauté quail over medium-high heat for 5 to 7 minutes or until brown and remove it to a paper towel–lined plate to drain. Remove all but 2 tablespoons of drippings from the pan. Gradually whisk reserved flour into the drippings and cook over medium heat for 3 minutes, or until golden brown. Whisk in chicken broth and continue to whisk until the mixture is smooth. Add quail, reduce heat, and simmer 20 minutes or until quail is done through. Stir occasionally to prevent scorching. Serve for breakfast with hot grits or for dinner with steaming hot rice and yams.

2 to 3 servings

Turkey Notes: When purchasing a turkey allow 1 pound of uncooked turkey per person. This allows for generous servings and some leftovers. If selecting fresh turkey, purchase no further than two days in advance, unless it is vacuum sealed with an expiration date. If electing to use a frozen turkey, allow a defrosting time of 24 hours per 5 pounds of turkey. Plan ahead—a 20-pound turkey could take 4 days to defrost. Thaw a frozen turkey in its original wrapper by placing it in a shallow pan on the bottom shelf of the refrigerator.

To stuff or not to stuff, that is the question. I prefer not to stuff turkey because the new, leaner turkeys are produced with more white meat, which requires less cooking time than dark meat. Also, a stuffed turkey must be roasted an additional 30 minutes to cook the stuffing. As a result, in an attempt to cook until the stuffing is done, you risk a dry, overcooked turkey. A few years ago, consumers were warned of the health risks associated with cooking a stuffed turkey. Experts now agree that those risks can be significantly reduced by taking the proper precautions. However, if you decide to stuff anyway, here are some rules of thumb: If you prepare your stuffing ahead of time, store wet and dry ingredients separately and combine them just before stuffing the bird. Stuff the turkey immediately before cooking. In addition to testing the bird's temperature, test the stuffing's temperature before serving (it should be 165°F). Use ¾ cup of stuffing per pound of turkey and do not overstuff or it will take longer to cook, resulting in overcooked turkey and packy dressing.

You can dry roast your turkey by not adding additional liquid to the pan at the beginning of cooking time. To dry roast your turkey, place it breast side up on a rack in a large roasting pan. To prevent the turkey from browning too quickly while maintaining the meat's tenderness, cover the turkey with a loose tent of foil for the first 2 to 3½ hours of cooking, depending on turkey size.

Roast according to package directions or until thigh temperature on a meat thermometer reaches 175°F. To test temperature using a thermometer, insert the thermometer in the thickest part of the thigh, angle it toward the turkey body, but do not allow it to touch the bone. If testing the breast instead of the thigh, the temperature of the breast meat should be 165°F. Remove foil during the last hour and 15 minutes of cooking time to allow the turkey to brown. Dry roasting produces a golden brown and wonderfully crisp bird; this is especially true where the bird has been basted. However, I also enjoy a moist roasted turkey, which requires the addition of pan liquid at the very outset of cooking. It is not quite as crisp as the dry roasted turkey; however, it is deliciously tender, moist, and flavorful. The recipe that follows is for a moist roasted turkey.

ORANGE AND MAPLE-GLAZED TURKEY WITH PECAN DRESSING AND GIBLET GRAVY

1   15-pound turkey
2   tablespoons salt
1   tablespoon black pepper
¾   teaspoon ground paprika
1   cup onion, coarsely chopped
½   cup celery, coarsely chopped
2   large naval oranges, quartered
1½   cups orange juice, divided

¾   cup sherry, divided
1   cup softened butter
3   cups chicken broth
1   cup onion, sliced
½   cup celery, sliced to a ¼-inch thickness
1¾   cups maple blended syrup

Remove turkey from packaging. Remove giblets and neck; set aside for use in making Giblet Gravy (recipe follows). Wash the bird inside and out under cold running water. Pat the turkey dry and then place it breast side up in a roasting pan. Combine salt, black pepper, and paprika; use mixture to season the turkey inside and out. With breast side up, lift wings up toward the neck, and then fold wing tips beneath the back of the wings. Fill turkey cavities with onion, celery, and naval orange. Pull neck skin over vegetable and fruit stuffing and secure to the back of bird with a skewer. Next, combine 1 cup of the orange juice and ½ cup of the sherry and slowly fill body cavity with the mixture. Tie leg ends together, cover tightly with aluminum foil, and refrigerate overnight.

The next day, preheat oven to 325°F. Rub turkey all over with softened butter. Pour broth, ½ cup orange juice, and ¼ cup sherry in the bottom of the roasting pan. Add sliced onion and celery to the pan. Roast 3 to 3½ hours in preheated oven, basting frequently with pan juices. While turkey is roasting, prepare the giblet gravy according to the recipe, opposite. At the end of 3½ hours remove turkey from roasting pan (reserve pan juices for gravy) and set in a shallow pan lined with heavy-duty foil. Pour syrup over turkey and place pan in oven; roast for an additional hour, basting every fifteen minutes with syrup.

12 to 14 servings

GIBLET GRAVY

Turkey neck and giblets
4 cups chicken broth
1 celery stalk, coarsely chopped
1 onion, coarsely chopped

Pan drippings
3 cups flour
Salt and pepper to taste

During the turkey's last hour of roasting, place the neck and giblets (minus liver, which can make your gravy bitter) in a saucepan with the broth, celery, and onion. Bring to a boil, then reduce heat and simmer two hours. If you choose to add the liver, do so during the last half hour of boiling time to reduce bitterness. Remove giblets and neck from saucepan; when they are sufficiently cool to handle, chop giblets coarsely. Remove meat from neck and discard bones. Strain broth and set aside. Separate the fat from the drippings in the first roasting pan and set aside. Add 4 cups of the de-fatted drippings to strained giblet broth. Measure and add additional broth to equal 6 cups liquid. Return 4 tablespoons of the reserved drippings to cool roasting pan, stir in flour, blending until smooth. Add 6 cups liquid, stir well. Place pan over medium-high heat and cook, stirring constantly, until mixture comes to a boil and is thickened. Strain into a saucepan and stir in chopped giblets and neck meat. Simmer 10 minutes and add salt and pepper to taste.

Yields 6 cups

PECAN DRESSING

2 pans J.R.'s Skillet Cornbread
(page 236)
4½ tablespoons butter
2¾ cups coarsely chopped
pecans, divided

½ teaspoon ground ginger
¼ teaspoon nutmeg
½ cup Granny Smith apple, peeled,
cored, and coarsely chopped
½ cup chicken broth

Preheat oven to 350°F. Place cooled cornbread in a large mixing bowl and break it into pieces. Crumble the cornbread by rubbing it between your palms. Continue this process until all cornbread is completely crumbled. Place hands firmly on either side of the bowl and sift by rotating the bowl in rapid circular motions against the counter top. Large pieces of bread should spin to the top and be removed from the bowl and reserved for reprocessing. Repeat the crumbling and spinning process until crumbs are of uniform size. Repeat process with large pieces of bread removed from the bowl, and set aside.

Melt butter over medium-high heat, reduce heat to low, and sauté pecans for five minutes. Stir constantly to prevent scorching. Add ginger, nutmeg, and chopped apple; continue to stir. Add pecan mixture and chicken broth to the cornbread and toss lightly to mix. Place dressing in a lightly buttered 11½ × 7½ × 8½-inch baking pan and bake in a preheated oven for 30 to 35 minutes or until golden.

6 servings

The Department of Theatre Arts

Art is not simply works of art; it has the spirit that knows beauty, that has music in its soul and the color of sunsets in its handkerchief, that can dance on a flaming world and make the world dance too.

—W. E. B. Du Bois,
Trustee, Howard University

The Department of Theatre Arts (formerly the Department of Drama) evolved from an uncredited speech course, which by 1870 was expanded to include an annual oratorical contest. By 1874, students were receiving credit for the course, and by 1899, under the supervision of Coralie Franklin Cook, a graduate of Philadelphia's National School of Elocution and Oratory, course work included such training as position of the body, breathing, and tone inflection.

Ernest Everett Just established the first black college drama club in America at Howard University soon after he arrived in 1909 to teach English. The highly successful group gave annual performances at the Howard Theatre in Washington, D.C.

In 1919, soon after his appointment as head of the Department of Speech, Montgomery Gregory founded the Howard Players, and theatre at Howard bloomed. For the first time, dramatic art courses, including acting, character portrayal, costume design, and production management, were offered for credit. The department boasted its own costume rooms and scenery workshop.

Montgomery dreamed of a national Negro theatre, and his players specialized in plays of African-American life, often written by aspiring students or established black playwrights such as James Baldwin. One of the group's earliest productions was *The Death*

Dance, by Thelma Duncan, written in 1921 while Duncan was a student in Gregory's class. It was later published in *Plays of Negro Life,* edited by Gregory and Alain Locke and was presented in the Rankin Memorial Chapel in 1923 to help raise funding for a university theatre laboratory.

In 1949, Anne Cook became head of the drama department, and under her direction, the Howard Players became goodwill ambassadors, touring two plays throughout Norway, Sweden, Denmark, and Germany.

Owen Dodson succeeded Cook, and during his tenure the departments of drama, art, and music merged to form the College of Fine Arts. In 1960 the college moved into the newly erected Lulu Vere Childers Hall, adjacent to the Ira Aldridge Theatre. James Baldwin's *Amen Corner* premiered there in 1964 under Dodson's direction.

Montgomery Gregory would have been proud to know that in 1978 the European premiere of the Broadway musical *Raisin* was performed by the Department of Drama and the Department of Music. As more than forty Howard University actors, dancers, and singers regaled European audiences, an additional twenty of their classmates were receiving the Premiere Award for best production in the 1979 Dundalk International Maytime Festival. Gregory's dream, a national Negro Theatre, had become an international success!

ROASTED TURKEY WITH PORT GRAVY

1	15-pound turkey		¾	teaspoon ground paprika
2	tablespoons salt		1	cup sliced onion
1	tablespoon black pepper		2	cups tawny port wine, divided

Remove turkey from packaging. Remove giblets and neck; set aside for use in making Port Gravy (recipe follows). Wash the bird inside and out under cold running water. Pat the turkey dry and then place it breast side up in a roasting pan. Combine salt, black pepper, and paprika; use mixture to season the turkey inside and out. With breast side up, lift wings up toward the neck, and then fold wing tips beneath the back of the wings. Pull neck skin over neck and secure to the back of bird with a skewer. Fill turkey cavity with onion and slowly fill body cavity with 1 cup of the port wine. Truss leg ends, cover tightly with aluminum foil, and refrigerate overnight.

The next day, preheat oven to 325°F. Pour remaining port wine into a large, 11½ × 17-inch roasting pan. Place turkey in the oven with a meat thermometer in the thickest part of the thigh, pointing in toward the body without touching bone. Cover the turkey with a tent of aluminum foil, push the top of the thermometer through the foil, and roast for approximately 3½ to 3¾ hours in preheated oven. Remove foil tent during the last 1¼ hours of cooking time. Baste frequently with pan juices. Turkey is done when thigh temperature reaches 175°F or breast temperature reaches 165°F. When turkey is done remove it to a platter to rest—at this point the turkey's temperature will rise 5 to 10 degrees. Cover turkey with foil to keep it warm while you prepare the Port Gravy according to the recipe below.

14 servings

PORT GRAVY

Pan drippings (reserve fat)	3–4 cups chicken broth
⅔ cup all-purpose flour	Salt and pepper to taste

Remove fat from pan juices and reserve. Over medium-high heat bring mixture to a boil while scraping up brown bits. Boil mixture until reduced by about half. In a 2½- to 3-quart heavy saucepan whisk together ½ cup reserved fat and flour and cook roux over moderately low heat, whisking, for 3 minutes. Add port mixture and 3 cups of the broth in a steady stream, whisking to prevent lumps, and bring gravy to a boil, whisking constantly. Simmer gravy, whisking frequently, for 5 minutes, or until thickened. If gravy is too thick, add additional broth. Season gravy with salt and pepper to taste. Transfer gravy to a heated sauceboat.

8 servings

RUM AND RAISIN-GLAZED HAM

1	7- to 8-pound fully cooked, cured ham	¼	teaspoon ground cloves
½	cup firmly packed brown sugar	⅓	cup raisins
		⅓	cup dark rum

Preheat oven to 350°F. Remove most of any skin attached to the ham with a sharp knife. Leave a collar of skin around the shank end of the bone and a ⅓-inch layer of fat on the ham. With a sharp knife score the fat layer with diamonds. Bake the ham on a rack in a roasting pan for 55 minutes. Combine remaining ingredients in a saucepan over medium-high heat, cook and stir the mixture until sugar melts. Use a spoon to spread the glaze over the ham, and bake the ham for 30 to 35 minutes more, or until the glaze browns. Transfer the ham to a platter, and let the ham stand for 15 minutes before carving.

8 servings

SMOTHERED PORK MEDALLIONS AND GRAVY

12	1-inch pork tenderloin medallions	⅓	cup onions, diced
	Seasoning Blend *(see recipe on page 196)*	¼	cup green peppers, diced
1	cup all-purpose flour	2	tablespoons celery, diced
3	tablespoons vegetable oil	1	teaspoon garlic, minced
2	tablespoons unsalted butter	1	tablespoon fresh thyme
		2–4	tablespoons all-purpose flour
		3	cups unsalted chicken broth

Wash pork medallions under cold running water, pat dry, season to taste with Seasoning Blend and set aside. Next, combine the flour with 1 tablespoon of the Seasoning Blend, dredge the medallions in the flour mixture, and shake away any excess flour. Place vegetable oil in a large, cast-iron skillet and heat over medium-high heat until it just begins to smoke. Reduce temperature to medium; add pork medallions to the pan while taking care not to crowd. Brown for 3 to 4 minutes on each side and remove from the pan to a paper towel–lined plate to drain. Add butter to the saucepan and melt over medium heat, add onions, and cook for 1 minute before adding the green bell pepper, celery, and garlic. Add thyme and cook over low heat for 5 minutes, until the onion is tender.

Add the flour and cook, stirring constantly, until the flour is golden brown. Add the chicken broth while whisking. The gravy will thicken as it comes to a boil. Return the pork medallions to the pan, reduce heat to low, and simmer for 5 minutes. Season the gravy with additional seasoning blend to taste.

6 servings

SEASONING BLEND

¼	cup salt	½	teaspoon cayenne pepper
¼	cup paprika	1	tablespoon dried thyme
¼	cup onion powder	1	teaspoon ground cumin
2	tablespoons garlic powder		Pinch of chili powder

Combine the above ingredients and mix well. Store the seasoning mix in a tightly covered, opaque container until ready to use.

Yields approximately 1 cup

HOWARD UNIVERSITY STAR: Roxie Roker, best known for her role as Helen Willis on the television sitcom *The Jeffersons,* graduated from Howard University in 1952. She was actively involved with the Howard Players and in Alpha Kappa Alpha Sorority, America's first black Greek-letter sorority. A gifted stage actress, in 1974 she won an Obie Award and was also nominated for a Tony for her performance as Mattie Williams in *The River Niger.*

PORK BUTT ROAST

1 6-pound pork butt roast	1 tablespoon olive oil
5 cloves garlic, mashed	1 large onion
2 teaspoons dried oregano	1 teaspoon salt
1 teaspoon ground black pepper	¼ teaspoon ground nutmeg
	¼ teaspoon cumin
1 tablespoon all-purpose flour	½ teaspoon ground allspice

Wash roast under cold running water and pat dry. Cut 10 to 12 ¼-inch marinating slits all over the roast. Combine remaining ingredients in a food processor and puree. Rub mixture all over the roast, wrap tightly in plastic wrap, and refrigerate overnight. The next day, place the roast fat side up on a rack in a shallow roasting pan and bake at 325°F for 3½ hours.

8 to 10 servings

GROUND BEEF CHILI

2 pounds lean ground beef	¼ teaspoon dried oregano
1 large green bell pepper, coarsely chopped	1 bay leaf
1 medium onion, coarsely chopped	1 fresh jalapeño pepper, seeded and minced, optional
3 cloves garlic, minced	2 14½-ounce cans chopped tomatoes, undrained
4 tablespoons chili powder	¼ cup beef broth
½ teaspoon cumin	1 16-ounce can pinto beans, drained
2 teaspoons paprika	

Cook meat, green bell pepper, onion, and garlic in a large pot over high heat until the meat is brown and the vegetables tender. Stir frequently to prevent scorching. Stir in chili powder and cook an additional minute, stirring frequently. Add cumin, paprika, oregano, bay leaf, and jalapeño pepper. Stir tomatoes, their liquid, and beef broth into the mixture and bring to a boil. Reduce heat to low; cover the pot, and simmer 45 minutes, stirring occasionally. Stir in beans, cover, and simmer an additional 15 minutes. Serve hot with corn muffins. Suggested Toppings: shredded Cheddar cheese, sour cream, green onions, chopped fresh jalapeño peppers.

6 servings

BLACK BEAN CHILI

1	tablespoon olive oil	1½	teaspoons garlic powder
2	pounds boneless, skinless chicken, cut into small cubes	1¼	teaspoons ground cumin
½	cup chopped onions	¾	teaspoon oregano leaves
3	cloves garlic, finely minced	⅛	teaspoon ground cayenne pepper
1	cup chicken broth	1	14½-ounce can diced tomatoes
1	fresh jalapeño pepper, seeded and chopped (optional)	1	19-ounce can black beans, undrained

Heat the olive oil in a large saucepan over medium-high heat. Add chicken, onions, and garlic, and sauté for 4 to 5 minutes. Stir in broth, jalapeño, if desired, and spices. Stir to mix and simmer 15 minutes. Stir in diced tomatoes and black beans; simmer an additional 5 minutes.

6 servings

OLD SCHOOL POT ROAST

1	3- to 4-pound beef roast	¼	cup burgundy wine
	Seasoning Blend *(see recipe*	3	cups unsalted beef broth
	on page 196)	2	carrots, sliced on the diagonal
4	slices bacon	2	bay leaves
1	large onion, sliced	½	teaspoon peppercorns
2	cloves garlic, minced	¼	teaspoon ground allspice
	Flour	2	tablespoons Worcestershire sauce

Preheat the oven to 300°F. Wash the roast under cold running water, pat dry, season to taste with Seasoning Blend and set aside. Render fat from the bacon in a large skillet placed over medium-high heat, but do not fry the bacon until crisp. Add onion and sauté until the onion is tender. Remove bacon and add the garlic. Dust the roast with flour and brown on all sides in the bacon drippings. Put meat on a rack in a Dutch oven. Deglaze the skillet by adding burgundy wine and scraping the bottom to release sediment and pan juices. Pour the mixture over the roast. Add remaining ingredients, cover tightly, and bake in preheated oven for approximately 3 hours. Serve with gravy made from pan drippings (below).

6 to 8 servings

MUSHROOM GRAVY

	Pan drippings (reserve fat)	1	cup sliced mushrooms
⅔	cup all-purpose flour		Salt and pepper to taste
3–4	cups hot beef broth		

Separate fat from pan juices and reserve. Over medium-high heat, bring mixture to a boil while scraping up the brown bits of sediment from the bottom of the pan. Boil mixture until reduced by half. In a 2½- to 3-quart saucepan, whisk together ½ cup of the reserved fat and flour and cook roux over moderately low heat, whisking 3 minutes. (If you have insufficient reserved fat, add some vegetable oil.) Add three cups of the broth in a steady stream, whisking constantly to prevent lumps. Add mushrooms and continue to whisk frequently while cooking for 5 minutes, or until thickened. If gravy is too thick add additional broth or water. Season gravy with salt and pepper to taste. Transfer gravy to a warm gravy server.

6 to 8 servings

SLOW-COOKED RUMP ROAST

Rump roast is an ideal cut of meat for slow cooking and makes an excellent pot roast. When selecting a roast for cooking, look for a bright red cut of meat that is firm and springy to the touch. The carrots are very important because their natural sweetness mellows the acidity of the tomatoes. This dish is excellent with rice and corn muffins.

1	3½-pound boneless rump roast	¼	teaspoon dried basil
2	tablespoons olive oil	2	bay leaves
1	medium-size onion, diced	2	envelopes dry onion soup (1 20-ounce box)
4	cloves garlic, minced	1	cup unsalted beef broth
1	28-ounce can diced tomatoes, undrained	¼	cup burgundy
1	teaspoon oregano	½	pound baby carrots
¾	teaspoon cumin	½	pound mushrooms, sliced
½	teaspoon black pepper	2	tablespoons cornstarch
¼	teaspoon dried rosemary	¼	cup cold water

Wash pot roast under cold running water and pat dry. Place olive oil in a nonstick skillet and brown the roast over medium-high heat. While meat is browning, combine onion, garlic, and tomatoes in an electric crock pot. Add roast and remaining ingredients, except carrots, mushrooms, cornstarch, and water. Stir mixture to blend. Cover slow cooker and cook on high for 8 to 10 hours. During the last hour of cooking, remove bay leaf from crock pot and remove beef to a platter. De-fat and purée broth in batches. Return purée to crock pot, add carrots, and cook an additional hour. During the last 15 minutes of cooking time add mushrooms. If you desire thicker gravy, combine cornstarch and cold water, mix well. Add cornstarch mixture to the crock pot, cover pot, and cook, stirring occasionally, for 15 minutes. Slice beef against the grain and serve over rice with gravy.

8 servings

ELEGANT FILET MIGNON

Candlelight, a little wine, and the sounds of Donald Byrd and the Blackbyrds create the perfect ambience for an intimate dinner with old classmates and friends. Open the yearbook and let the stories flow with the warmth of a smooth burgundy. And ask, "Do you remember . . . ?"

4	filet mignon, 1½-inches thick		2	tablespoons shallots, finely chopped
	Salt and freshly ground		3	ounces brandy
	pepper to taste		4	tablespoons butter
1½	teaspoons olive oil		1	tablespoon heavy cream
2	large cloves of garlic,		3	tablespoons parsley, minced
	quartered			

Wash meat under cold running water, pat dry, and season to taste with salt and pepper. In a large skillet, heat olive oil over medium-high heat. Add garlic, shallots, and the filets. Sauté steaks for approximately 3 to 4 minutes on each side. The steak is medium-rare when small drops of red juice form on the steak's surface. Transfer steak to a warm platter and keep warm. Remove garlic from skillet, add brandy, and reduce by half. Add butter and stir until melted, add cream, and warm through. Pour sauce on filets and garnish with parsley.

4 servings

Note: If you do not plan to cook your beef within 8 hours of purchase, remove it from store packaging, wrap it lightly in wax paper to allow air to circulate, and store in the coldest part of your refrigerator for up to 3 days. For longer storage, place the meat in airtight foil or freezer wrap and freeze it for up to 6 months.

Grill Notes: To prevent sticky messes, spray the grate of your grill with nonstick cooking spray before you grill. If you find some food has stuck to your gas grill grates, close the lid after you finish cooking and turn the burner on high for 10 minutes; this will burn off any food that has stuck to the grate or has dripped to the bottom of the grill. When building a charcoal fire, calculate the amount of charcoal required by first determining how hot you want your fire. If you want a very hot fire, spread a double layer of briquettes across the grate. A medium-hot fire requires a tightly packed single layer. The more space allowed between each briquette, the lower the heat from the fire. To light your fire, form the charcoal into a pyramid or a starter chimney, add lighter fluid according to manufacturer's directions, and light. (I prefer to use an electric starter to avoid the fumes and aftertaste of lighter fluid.)

To estimate the temperature of coals, hold your hand palm side down, approximately 4 inches above the coals. A medium-hot grill will allow you to hold your hand comfortably over the coals for 2 to 3 seconds. A medium grill will allow you to hold your hand over the coals for 3 to 4 seconds.

Always preheat the grill rack because food placed on a cold rack over hot coals will stick and char. Allow twenty minutes to preheat a charcoal grill and 10 to 15 minutes for a gas grill. Remember, grilling requires constant attention and full concentration. It only takes a few moments of inattentiveness to destroy a morning's work.

To test for doneness, place a small slit in the center of the steaks and note the inside color: red indicates rare; pink is medium; gray, well done.

Cold salads are great accompaniments because they can be prepared in advance and brought out and served without any additional preparation. However, it wouldn't be barbecue without beans—so make them ahead of time and reheat just prior to serving. Or select hot items that can be prepared, warmed, or kept warm on the grill. Fresh corn, for instance, is irresistible when prepared on the grill! Try the Zesty Grilled Corn on the Cob recipe on page 147.

Fresh fish is another delicious grill favorite. Select firm-fleshed fish like salmon, halibut, sea bass, tuna, or swordfish. Oil your grilling grate and leave the skin on to prevent the fish from sticking to the grill or falling apart. Shrimp and scallops are also perfect grill selections. However, nothing beats a succulent, well-grilled steak with all the fixings!

GRILLED T-BONE STEAK AND PORTOBELLO MUSHROOMS

Long prized for its tenderness and flavor, the T-bone steak is a cut above others and perfect for the grill. When selecting a steak check for marbeling (intramuscular fat). Prime, the choicest cut, has the most marbeling. However, if prime is unavailable, look for USDA top choice or choice.

2 1¼- to 1½-pound prime or top choice T-bone steaks, 1½ inches thick	1 tablespoon olive oil 1¼ teaspoons salt 2 teaspoons freshly ground pepper

The night before grilling, wash steaks under cold running water and pat dry. Slash the fat edge of the steak at 1-inch intervals to keep the steaks flat on the grill. Do not cut into the lean meat. Rub steaks with olive oil, wrap loosely in wax paper, and place in the coldest part of the refrigerator. The next day, combine salt and pepper, mix well, and set aside to season steaks. Build a pile of charcoal briquettes on the bottom of your grill, ignite, and allow to burn down until the coals are lightly covered with gray ash.*

Spread coals evenly. Replace cooking grate 4 to 6 inches above coals and allow it to heat for 15 minutes before seasoning steaks and placing them in the center of the grate. Close lid and grill steaks 5 to 7 minutes before turning. Grill an additional 7 minutes or until meat thermometer inserted into the thickest part of the steaks registers 130°F. Remove steaks to large steak platter and allow to sit 5 minutes for medium-rare steaks; this allows the juices to settle and facilitates the steaks' tenderness. For medium steaks, cook an additional 5 to 7 minutes.

2 servings

---

*If using a gas grill, heat all burners on high for 15 to 20 minutes before arranging steaks on the grill.

GRILLED PORTOBELLO MUSHROOMS

½	cup olive oil		2	teaspoons Worcestershire sauce
⅓	cup balsamic vinegar			Juice of 1 lemon
3	cloves minced garlic		4	large Portobello mushrooms

Make the marinade by combining the first five ingredients. Remove stems from mushroom caps and marinate the caps for 15 minutes. Grill the mushrooms over a medium fire for 4 to 5 minutes on each side.

4 servings

MAKE MINE A PORTERHOUSE AND SCOTCH

2	16-ounce porterhouse steaks, 1 inch thick		1	teaspoon fresh shallots, chopped
2	ounces Scotch whiskey		½	teaspoon garlic, minced
¼	teaspoon fresh dill, chopped			Salt and pepper to taste

Wash steaks under cold running water and pat dry. Slash the fat edge of the steak at 1-inch intervals to keep the steaks flat on the grill. Do not cut into the lean meat. Combine next 4 ingredients in a shallow, non-reactive dish or a large, heavy-duty, zip-top plastic bag. Add steaks, seal tightly, and refrigerate for 1 hour. Turn once.

Build a pile of charcoal briquettes on the bottom of your grill, ignite, and allow to burn down until the coals are lightly covered with gray ash.* Spread coals evenly, replace cooking grate 4 to 6 inches above coals, and allow to heat for 15 minutes before seasoning steaks and placing them in the center of the grate. Close lid and grill steaks 5 to 7 minutes on each side or until desired doneness is reached. Remove steaks to large steak platter and allow to sit five minutes before serving.

2 servings

*If using a gas grill, heat all burners on high for 15 to 20 minutes before arranging steaks on the grill.

GRILLED FLANK STEAK

1	¾-pound flank steak	3	garlic cloves, minced
¼	cup fresh lemon juice	2	teaspoons dried marjoram
½	cup olive oil	2	teaspoons Tabasco sauce
¼	cup sherry	½	teaspoon salt
2	tablespoons onion, grated	½	teaspoon pepper

Wash flank steak under cold running water, pat dry, and set aside. Combine next seven ingredients in a shallow, non-reactive dish or a large, heavy-duty, zip-top plastic bag; add flank steak, tightly seal, and refrigerate for 8 hours or overnight, turning the steak occasionally. Remove steak from marinade, discard marinade, and season steak with salt and pepper. Grill over medium-high heat (350 to 400°F) for 4 to 6 minutes on each side or to desired degree of doneness. Allow to stand 5 minutes before cutting steak into thin strips by slicing it diagonally across the grain.

6 servings

OVEN-BAKED BRISKET

Is it too rainy or cold to grill outdoors? Try this flavorful, oven-baked brisket.

1	4½-pound untrimmed beef brisket	1	teaspoon salt
½	cup vegetable oil	2	teaspoons ground black pepper
3	cloves garlic, finely minced	2	tablespoons Worcestershire sauce
¼	cup cider vinegar	1	¼-ounce envelope dry onion soup
¼	cup ketchup	½	cup water
		½	cup orange juice

Brown the brisket in half of the hot vegetable oil for 5 minutes on each side. Place the brisket in a lightly greased 13- × 19-inch pan and set aside while preparing cooking sauce. Combine the remaining ingredients, including the remaining vegetable oil, mix well, and pour over the brisket. Cover the pan and bake in a preheated 350°F oven for 1 hour. Baste the brisket, reduce heat to 300°F, and bake an additional hour. Degrease the pan drippings and pour over brisket prior to serving.

4 to 6 servings

BARBECUED SPARE RIBS
WITH HONEY-MUSTARD BARBECUE SAUCE

2   sides (6 to 8 pounds) pork spare ribs
⅓   cup firmly packed brown sugar
¼   cup garlic powder
2   tablespoons onion powder
2   tablespoons paprika
2   teaspoons lemon pepper

2   tablespoons ground black pepper
2½ tablespoons ground red pepper
2   teaspoons salt
⅓   teaspoon ground cumin
1¾ teaspoons ground allspice
½   teaspoon ground nutmeg
    Nonstick cooking spray

One day prior to grilling, wash ribs under cold running water, pat dry, place on a rimmed cookie sheet, and set aside. Combine the remaining spices, mix well, and rub into both sides of the ribs. Cover tightly with aluminum foil and refrigerate overnight.

The next day build a hot white fire in grill, spray grate with non-stick cooking spray and set it 6 inches above hot coals for 10 to 15 minutes before placing ribs on the grill. Cook ribs for 20 minutes, turn and cook an additional 20 minutes, or until done. Test ribs by slicing away a riblet at the thickest end of the slab and ensuring that it is cooked through. Either brush ribs with sauce while they are cooking or serve on the side. Serve with Dilled Deli Potato Salad on page 124 and Country Cole Slaw on page 122.

6 servings

HONEY MUSTARD BARBECUE SAUCE

1½ cups prepared smoked barbecue sauce	2 tablespoons Dijon-style mustard
¼ cup brown sugar	½ stick (4 tablespoons) butter
¼ cup honey	¼ tablespoon allspice

Combine the above ingredients in a medium-size saucepan and bring to a boil; reduce heat and simmer 15 minutes. Serve hot with grilled ribs.

8 servings

GRILLED RIBS WITH HOMEMADE BARBECUE SAUCE

This is an old-fashioned recipe that calls for parboiling the ribs. This cooking method results in much juicier and more tender ribs.

⅓ cup onions, minced	1 teaspoon salt
¼ cup green pepper, finely chopped	1 teaspoon paprika
1¼ cups tomato puree	1 teaspoon chili powder
3 tablespoons white vinegar	½ teaspoon red pepper
3 tablespoons Worcestershire sauce	¼ teaspoon ground cinnamon
	Pinch of ground cloves
	2 sides (6 to 8 pounds) pork spare ribs

Make a basting sauce by combining the above ingredients except ribs in a large kettle, and bringing the mixture to a quick boil. Reduce heat and simmer 30 minutes. In a separate kettle, parboil ribs 30 minutes. Place in sauce to marinate for 30 minutes before grilling.

Build a white-hot fire in grill, spray grate with non-stick cooking spray, and set it 6 inches above hot coals for 10 to 15 minutes before placing ribs on the grill. Cook ribs for 15 minutes, turn and cook an additional 15 minutes, or until done. Serve with Dilled Deli Potato Salad on page 124 and Country Coleslaw on page 122.

6 servings

GRILLED BABY BACK RIBS

These ribs are tasty enough to eat without sauce. However, if you prefer one, try the Honey-Mustard Barbecue Sauce on pages 206–7.

2	sides (6 to 8 pounds) baby back pork spare ribs	2	teaspoons coarsely ground black pepper
3	tablespoons firmly packed light brown sugar	1	teaspoon kosher salt
2	tablespoons garlic powder	1	teaspoon ground cumin
2¼	teaspoons ground paprika	¾	teaspoon ground allspice
2	teaspoons lemon pepper	⅛	teaspoon ground cinnamon

The day before serving, wash ribs under cold running water and set aside to drain. Combine the remaining ingredients and mix well to form a dry rub. Place ribs on a rimmed baking sheet, evenly sprinkle the ribs with the dry rub, and rub it into the meat. Tightly cover and refrigerate overnight.

Before grilling, coat grill rack with nonstick cooking spray and prepare a medium fire in the grill. Place grill rack 6 inches above the heat and grill 25 minutes before turning ribs and grilling an additional 25 to 30 minutes, or until cooked through. These ribs are excellent with Country Cole Slaw (page 122), Zesty Grilled Corn on the Cob (page 147) and Fried Apples (page 173).

6 servings

GRILLED LAMB

1   7- to 9-pound leg of lamb, boned, butterflied, and cut into 4 sections. (Have butcher remove silver skin and excess fat.)
2   tablespoons chili sauce
2   onions
12 large cloves garlic
5   tablespoons fresh rosemary leaves, minced

5   tablespoons fresh sage leaves, minced
3   tablespoons fresh mint leaves, minced
1   teaspoon cumin
¾   cup olive oil
¼   cup Worcestershire sauce
2   tablespoons lime juice

Wipe lamb with a clean damp cloth and set aside. Process the remaining ingredients to form a paste. Spread mixture on both sides of the lamb. Place lamb in a large dish or roaster and refrigerate overnight. The next day, place lamb on a medium grill and cook to medium rare, 7 to 8 minutes on each side, or to desired degree of doneness. Transfer to a cutting board and allow to stand 5 minutes before slicing to serve.

8 to 10 servings

GRILLED SALMON

⅓   cup lime juice (juice from 2 limes)
2   tablespoons olive oil
½   teaspoon salt
1   tablespoon grated ginger

4   salmon steaks (1½ pounds total), each ¾-inch thick
¼   cup green onion, chopped
1   tablespoon water
¼   teaspoon honey

Combine lime juice, oil, salt, and grated ginger in a small bowl and mix to blend. Place salmon in a shallow dish. Pour ¼ cup lime juice mixture over fish; turn to coat. Refrigerate 10 minutes, turning once.

Reserve the remaining mixture for sauce. Prepare a charcoal grill with hot coals, or heat a gas grill or broiler to high. Position the grill rack 6 inches from coals or broiler pan 3 inches from heat.

Stir green onion, water, and honey into reserved lime juice mixture. Bring to a quick boil in a small saucepan.

Grease grill rack or rack of a shallow roasting pan. Place salmon on rack or in pan. Drizzle with half of lime juice mixture from marinade dish. Grill over hot coals on covered grill 2 minutes per side or until cooked through, or broil 4 minutes per side. Serve salmon with remaining lime juice mixture.

4 servings

OVEN-ROASTED CHICKEN BREASTS AND SEASONED RICE

4 chicken breasts	½ cup chicken broth
1¼ teaspoons salt	4 tablespoons butter, divided
1 teaspoon white pepper	Uncooked rice
½ teaspoon onion powder	½ cup green onions, including tops, sliced thin
¼ teaspoon paprika	

Preheat oven to 350°F. Wash chicken breasts; remove and discard excess fat. Combine salt, pepper, onion powder, and paprika, mix well and use to season chicken. Place seasoned breasts into a baking dish with chicken broth. Place one tablespoon of butter on each breast. Cover with foil and bake in preheated oven for 1 hour. Remove foil and continue to bake an additional ½ hour or until chicken breasts are browned and tender. Use pan drippings to make seasoned rice by combining with additional broth or water to make sufficient liquid to make 4 servings cooked according to package directions. Add sliced green onions during the last 5 minutes of cooking.

4 servings

Donald Byrd and the Blackbyrds

While serving on the faculty, Donald Byrd founded the Howard University Jazz Studies program in the early 1970s. In 1974 he assembled players from the music department to form the Blackbyrds. The group was named after *Black Byrd*, his hit fusion album of the previous year. "Walking in Rhythm," was the group's first major hit, followed by "Happy Music," "Do It, Fluid," and that silky smooth jazz hit, "Summer Love." Original members of the Blackbyrds included percussionist Pericles "Perk" Jacobs, Jr., drummer Keith Killgo, keyboardist Kevin Toney, reeds player Allan Barnes, bassist Joe Hall, and guitarist Barney Perry. In his spare time Byrd pursued a law degree, and he received his juris doctorate from Howard in 1976.

BROWNED OYSTERS

1 quart fresh oysters, shucked	Juice of one lemon
1½ tablespoons flour	Worcestershire sauce
5 tablespoons butter, divided	Salt and pepper to taste
1 tablespoon minced shallot	

Drain oysters and reserve their liquid. Dredge oysters in flour and brown in 2 tablespoons of butter. Remove oysters and cooking juices from the pan; reserve cooking juices. Add remaining butter and melt over medium-high heat. Add shallot and cook for 2 to 3 minutes. Whisk in flour and brown while continuously whisking, 3 to 5 minutes. Add reserved liquid and stir to blend. Cook an additional 2 to 3 minutes. Add lemon juice, a dash of Worcestershire sauce, and oysters and their pan juice. Add salt and pepper to taste and serve over a bed of steaming hot white rice.

4 servings

SEAFOOD STEW

¼ cup olive oil	1 tablespoon Worcestershire sauce
1 large onion, chopped fine	1 cup water
1 large green bell pepper, chopped fine	1 bay leaf
5 large garlic cloves, minced fine	2 pounds monkfish (dark membrane removed), cut into 2-inch pieces
1 jalapeño pepper, seeded and chopped fine	2 pounds unshelled mussels
45 ounces (3 15-oz cans) tomato sauce	2 pounds large shrimp, peeled and deveined
	2 pints cooked crabmeat
	2 tablespoons fresh parsley, minced

Sauté onions, bell peppers, garlic, and jalapeño in olive oil. Add tomato sauce, and next three ingredients. Stir sauce until it is smooth. Cover pot and simmer 30 minutes. Increase heat to medium-high. Stir in monkfish and cook 2 minutes. Stir in mussels; cover and cook 2 minutes. Stir in shrimp; cover and cook 2 minutes or until mussels open and the shrimp and fish turn opaque. Discard any unopened mussels; stir in crabmeat and warm through. Garnish with parsley before serving with plenty of warm, crusty Cuban, Italian, or French bread.

6 servings

FRIED TROUT

1 egg	¼ teaspoon sugar
1 cup water	⅛ teaspoon cayenne pepper
½ cup flour	2 rainbow or brook trout, dressed and butterflied
¾ cup corn meal	½ cup vegetable oil
1 teaspoon onion salt	Lemon wedges
½ teaspoon salt	Chopped flat leaf parsley
¼ teaspoon ground white pepper	

Combine egg and water and slowly whisk in flour and corn meal. Add onion salt, salt, ground white pepper, sugar, and cayenne pepper. Place prepared fish in batter while oil is heating.

In heavy skillet (preferably cast-iron or nonstick), heat oil over medium-high heat until ½ teaspoon batter dropped into it sizzles and begins to brown. Fry fish for 3 minutes on each side. Remove and drain on paper towels.

Garnish with lemon slices and chopped parsley.

4 servings

GRAIN

Toni Morrison

I want to write for people like me, which is to say black people, curious people, demanding people—people who can't be faked, people who don't need to be patronized, people who have very, very high criteria.

—Toni Morrison

Toni Morrison was born Chloe Anthony Wofford to working-class parents in Lorain, Ohio. She displayed her literary inclination early, with adolescent reading interests that included Austen, Tolstoy, Dostoyevski, and Flaubert. Her mother and her father, George, a hardworking welder, and his wife Ramah shared tales from Southern black folklore with their daughter. After graduating with honors from Lorain High School in 1949, Morrison attended Howard, where she majored in English with a minor in classics. She also joined the university's highly acclaimed theatre group, the Howard Players.

Morrison received her master's degree from Cornell University in 1955 and taught for a while at Texas Southern University in Houston before joining the Howard faculty in 1957, where she crossed paths with poet Amiri Baraka (at that time called LeRoi Jones), Andrew Young, Stokely Carmichael, and Claude Brown, author of the classic *Manchild in the Promised Land.*

Morrison joined a small writers' group for which she wrote a short story loosely based on a childhood acquaintance who prayed to God for blue eyes. This story was later expanded into her first novel, *The Bluest Eye,* published in 1970. In 1964, she accepted employment with a major New York City publisher and worked as an editor there until 1984, while simultaneously writing increasingly acclaimed novels and occasionally teaching and lecturing at prestigious universities. Her novels include *Sula* (1973), *Song of Solomon* (1977), *Tar Baby* (1981), *Beloved* (1987), *Jazz* (1992), and *Paradise* (1998). *Song of Solomon* won the National Book Critics Circle Award and the American Academy and Institute of Arts and Letters Award; *Beloved* won the 1988 Pulitzer Prize for fiction. In 1993 Morrison received the Nobel Prize in Literature. Morrison is also the author of *Dreaming Emmett,* a play based on the racist murder of Emmett Till.

In 1980, President Jimmy Carter appointed Toni Morrison to the National Council on the Arts. While accepting her Pulitzer, Morrison had commented, "I take teaching as seriously as I do my writing," and in 1987, she was named the Robert F. Goheen Professor in the Council of Humanities at Princeton University, becoming the first black woman writer to hold a named chair at an ivy league university.

In 1993, she added another significant honor to an already long list: Toni Morrison became the first African-American woman to receive the Nobel Prize in Literature.

SWEET POTATO BREAD

The terms *sweet potato* and *yam* are used interchangeably to describe a sweet starchy tuber. True yams, however, are distinguished from sweet potatoes by their dark skin and sweet, moist orange flesh.

2 eggs, well beaten	1¼ teaspoons ground nutmeg
1½ cups sugar	Pinch of allspice
½ cup vegetable oil	1 teaspoon baking soda
⅓ cup water	½ teaspoon salt
2 teaspoons vanilla extract	1 cup cold mashed sweet potatoes
1¾ cups all-purpose flour	½ cup golden raisins
1¼ teaspoons cinnamon	½ cup coarsely chopped walnuts

Preheat oven to 350°F. Grease 2 1-pound coffee cans and set aside. Combine eggs, sugar, oil, water, and vanilla. Mix well. In a separate bowl, combine dry ingredients; mix well and add to the egg mixture. Stir until just mixed. Add mashed sweet potatoes, raisins, and nuts.

Divide batter between prepared coffee cans and bake for 55 to 60 minutes or until a tester inserted into the center of the bread comes out clean. Place coffee cans on wire racks to cool for 10 minutes before turning loaves out and allowing them to completely cool.

Yields 2 loaves

JALAPEÑO AND CHEESE CORN MUFFINS

1½	cups yellow corn meal		½	cup sour cream
3	teaspoons baking powder		¾	cup grated cheese
½	teaspoon salt		½	cup fresh jalapeño peppers, chopped
1	small can cream-style corn		¼	cup red bell pepper, chopped
3	eggs, beaten		½	cup vegetable oil

Preheat oven to 450°F. Combine dry ingredients and mix well. Add remaining ingredients and mix to blend. Grease tins of one large muffin pan and place in preheated oven for 5 minutes. Remove tins and fill each cup with muffin mixture. Bake for 20 minutes or until golden.

1 dozen muffins

BACON AND SAGE CORN MUFFINS

	Vegetable oil		½	teaspoon salt
8	slices bacon		1	cup buttermilk
1½	cups yellow corn meal		2	eggs, lightly beaten
½	cup all-purpose flour		1½	cups cream-style corn
3	tablespoons sugar		½	cup fresh sage, finely chopped
1	tablespoon baking powder			

Preheat oven to 400°F. Grease a 12-muffin pan and set aside. Fry bacon until crisp and remove from pan to a paper towel–lined plate. Reserve pan drippings. Combine corn meal, flour, sugar, baking powder, and salt. Place buttermilk in a separate bowl and add ¼ cup bacon drippings (add vegetable oil to bacon drippings if necessary to yield ¼ cup). Add eggs to buttermilk mixture and mix well. Slowly add dry ingredients and mix until just moistened. Stir in corn, sage, and crumbled bacon. Fill muffin cups almost to the top, place in a preheated oven, and bake for 22 to 25 minutes until tester inserted into the center of a muffin comes out clean and the muffins are golden brown.

1 dozen muffins

Claude Brown

Claude Brown, born in 1937, grew up in a Harlem tenement on 146th Street and Eighth Avenue. His parents had moved from the South to New York, the "Promised Land," in search of a better life for their family, free from the burdens of racism. As Brown would later write, "Going to New York was good-bye to the cotton fields, good-bye to 'Massa Charlie,' good-bye to the chain gang, and, most of all, good-bye to those sunup-to-sundown working hours. One no longer had to wait to get to heaven to lay his burden down; burdens could be laid down in New York."

Life in New York brought serious challenges, too. Claude was expelled from school at eight, joined a street gang at nine, was shot at thirteen during a burglary, and sent to reform school at age fourteen. There he met psychologist Ernest Papanek, director of the Wiltwyck School for deprived and emotionally disturbed boys. Papanek encouraged the intelligent youngster to get an education, which eventually led Brown to Howard University in 1959, where Toni Morrison was one of his teachers.

During Brown's first year of college, Papanek encouraged him to write an article for *Dissent* magazine. That article caught the attention of a book editor who invited Brown to lunch. Claude Brown left with a book offer and a $2,000.00 advance. The book he wrote went on to become a classic. Based largely on his own life, *Manchild in the Promised Land,* is a disturbing account of a young man raised in the midst of Harlem's drug addicts, killers, and prostitutes. Published during the height of the civil rights movement and now required reading in many high schools and colleges, more than 4 million copies have been sold.

FRESH CORN MUFFINS

1½ cups unsifted all-purpose flour	1 cup whole kernel corn
½ cup yellow corn meal	1 cup table cream
1 tablespoon baking powder	¼ cup vegetable oil
½ teaspoon salt	1 large egg
	3 tablespoons honey

Preheat oven to 400°F. Generously grease a 9-muffin tin and set aside. In a large bowl, combine flour, corn meal, baking powder, and salt, mix well. Toss corn in corn meal mixture until it is well coated and scattered throughout. In a separate bowl, combine the cream, oil, egg, and honey and stir into the flour mixture. Divide the batter evenly among the prepared muffin cups. Bake 20 to 25 minutes until golden or a tester inserted into the center of a muffin comes out clean. Allow muffins to sit for 5 minutes before turning out onto a wire rack to cool.

9 muffins

BUTTERMILK CORN MUFFINS

According to folklore, a guest who is served cold bread may assume he or she is not welcome.

3	cups yellow corn meal	2	tablespoons melted shortening
2¼	teaspoons baking powder	⅓	cup melted butter
¾	teaspoon baking soda	2	cups buttermilk
1	teaspoon salt	2	unbeaten eggs

Preheat oven to 425°F. Lightly grease a 9-muffin tin and set aside. In a large mixing bowl, combine corn meal, baking powder, baking soda, and salt. Mix dry ingredients together thoroughly. Combine shortening, butter, buttermilk, and eggs. Make a well in the center of corn meal mixture and pour buttermilk mixture into the center of the well. Beat mixture until evenly moistened and spoon into muffin tins. Place in preheated oven and bake for 25 to 35 minutes until golden or a tester inserted into the center of a muffin comes out clean. Serve with plenty of rich country buttermilk.

9 muffins

Amiri Baraka (Le Roi Jones)

Baraka . . . stands with Wheatley, Douglass, Dunbar, Hughes, Hurston, Wright, and Ellison as one of the eight figures (in my opinion) who have significantly affected the course of African-American literary culture. His change of heart and head is testimony to his honesty, energy, and relentless search for meaning.

—Arnold Rampersad,
professor of literature, Princeton University

Amiri Baraka, one of the most prolific, gifted, and controversial writers of our time, was born Everett LeRoy Jones in Newark, New Jersey, on October 7, 1934. His father, Colt, was a postal supervisor and his mother, Anna Lois Jones, was a social worker. Jones attending Rutgers University for two years, then transferred to Howard, where he earned a bachelor's in English in 1954 and changed the spelling of his given name to Le Roi. Following a stint in the air force, he moved to Greenwich Village, where he immersed himself in its arts community, married Hettie Cohen, and co-edited a literary magazine with her, and founded Totem Press, which published works by Allen Ginsberg, Jack Kerouac, and other members of the "beat generation."

In 1961, his first volume of poetry, *Preface to a Twenty-Volume Suicide Note*, was published. Two racially charged plays, *The Slave* and *The Toilet*, followed in 1962. *Blues People: Negro Music in White America* was published in 1963. During the same year, he wrote and introduced *The Moderns: An Anthology of New Writing in America*. His star continued to rise and his reputation as a playwright was firmly established with *Dutchman*, which premiered at the Cherry Lane Theatre in New York on March 24, 1964, earning him an Obie Award for best off-Broadway play.

Following the assassination of Malcolm X in 1965, Baraka divorced his wife, left his former life, and moved to Harlem to help found the Black Arts Repertory Theater/School (BARTS). Although BARTS itself was short-lived, it gave rise to a number of similar schools throughout the nation, including California's Black House and the Spirithouse in Newark, also founded by Baraka. In 1967, he married African-American poet Sylvia Robinson (now Amina Baraka), and Spirithouse produced two of his plays that spoke out against police brutality: *Police* and *Arm Yrself or Harm Yrself*.

In 1968 *Black Fire: An Anthology of Afro-American Writing*, co-edited with Larry Neal, was published, and Baraka's play, *Home on the Range*, was produced and performed as a benefit for the Black Panther party. That year Jones converted to the Muslim religion and he changed his name to Imamu ("spiritual leader") Baraka. In 1968, he was living in

Newark, New Jersey, where he formed Kawaida, a Black Muslim organization with social, religious, and political goals for the improvement of the lives of African-Americans in Newark and throughout the nation. These continuing interests were manifest when he chaired the Committee for Unified Newark; founded and chaired the Congress of African People, a national Pan-Africanist organization; and was among the chief organizers of the National Black Political Convention in 1972.

In 1983, he and Amina Baraka edited *Confirmation: An Anthology of African-American Women,* which won an American Book Award from the Before Columbus Foundation. The *Autobiography of LeRoi Jones/Amiri Baraka* was published in 1984, and 1987 brought the publication of the Barakas' *The Music: Reflections on Jazz and Blues.*

His numerous literary prizes and honors include: fellowships from the Guggenheim Foundation and the National Endowment for the Arts, the PEN/Faulkner Award, the Rockefeller Foundation Award for Drama, the Langston Hughes Award from the City College of New York, and a lifetime achievement award from the Before Columbus Foundation. He is co-director, with his wife, of Kimako's Blues People, a community arts space in Newark, and he continues to write and work for political and social change. In 2001, he was named poet laureate of New Jersey.

HAM AND CHEESE MUFFINS

1½ cups flour	2 eggs, well beaten
2 teaspoons baking powder	¾ cup table cream
1 tablespoon sugar	½ cup milk
¼ teaspoon salt	3 tablespoons melted butter
½ cup wheat bran	½ cup coarsely grated Cheddar
¾ cup cooked ham, finely chopped	cheese

Preheat oven to 350°F. Butter a 12-muffin tin and set aside. Sift together flour, baking powder, sugar, and salt. Stir in bran, ham, and eggs. Combine cream, milk, and butter, mix well and add this milk mixture to the dry ingredients. Add cheese and stir gently, only until mixed. Divide batter among the muffin tins, filling them approximately ⅔ full. Bake in a preheated oven for approximately 25 minutes. Serve hot with butter.

1 dozen muffins

Valerie Wilson Wesley

Howard graduate and former executive editor of *Essence Magazine* Valerie Wilson Wesley is the author of many popular books, including an African-American mystery series set in the tough streets of Newark, New Jersey, and starring the smart cop-turned-private detective Tamara Hayle. A number of her novels have been best sellers, and *Ain't Nobody's Business If I Do* received the 2000 Award for Excellence in Adult Fiction from the Black Caucus of the American Library Association. She is also the author of *Freedom's Gifts: A Juneteenth Story,* a picture book for children, and *Where Do I Go From Here,* a novel for young adults, for which she received an American Library Association Best Book for Reluctant Readers citation. Her latest novel is *Always True to You in My Fashion.*

Wesley is married to noted screenwriter, playwright, and Howard graduate Richard Wesley, whose screenplays include *Native Son, Uptown Saturday Night, Let's Do It Again,* and *Mandela and De Klerk.*

WHOLE WHEAT MUFFINS

1 cup all-purpose flour	½ cup half-and-half
2½ teaspoons baking powder	½ cup milk
¼ teaspoon salt	2 tablespoons honey
1 cup whole-wheat flour	⅓ cup vegetable oil
½ cup packed brown sugar	⅓ cup pecans, chopped
2 eggs, lightly beaten	

Preheat oven to 350°F. Sift flour, baking powder, and salt into a large bowl. Add whole-wheat flour and brown sugar. Mix to combine. Next, in a separate bowl, combine eggs, half-and-half, milk, honey, and vegetable oil, mix well, and stir into dry ingredients until moistened. Fold in pecans. Fill 12 greased or paper-lined muffin cups ⅔ full, and bake in a preheated oven for 15 minutes or until golden and a tester inserted in the center of the muffin comes out clean. Allow muffins to sit 5 minutes before turning them out onto a wire rack to cool.

1 dozen muffins

Howard University Star

Bernice Johnson Reagon,
renowned musicologist and founder
of Sweet Honey in the Rock
(Sharon Farmer)

Bernice Johnson Reagon, founder of Sweet Honey in the Rock, the Grammy winning African-American female a cappella ensemble, took her Ph.D. at Howard University in 1975. Reagon was a member of the original SNCC Freedom Singers formed during the height of the 60s civil rights movement. The Freedom Singers brought a musical voice to the struggle for equality, singing such movement anthems as "We Shall Not Be Moved," as well as spirituals from the black church that amplified the cry for freedom. Dr. Reagon's impressive work continues to reflect her cultural pride and commitment to human equality and social justice.

The scholar, composer, singer, and activist—is the 2002–03 Cosby Chair Professor of Fine Arts at Spelman College in Atlanta, Georgia. The recipient of the 2003 Heinz Award for the Arts and Humanities for her work as a scholar and artist in African-American cultural history and music, Reagon is professor emeritus of history at American University and curator emeritus at the Smithsonian Institution's National Museum of American History in Washington, D.C.

Since its founding in 1973, Reagon continues to lead and perform with Sweet Honey in the Rock and has produced most of the group's recordings. Her work as a scholar and composer is reflected in publications and productions on African-American culture and history, including: a collection of essays entitled *If You Don't Go, Don't Hinder Me: The African-American Sacred Song Tradition* (U. of Nebraska Press, 2001); *We'll Understand It Better By and By: Pioneering African-American Gospel Composers* (Smithsonian Press, 1992); *We Who Believe in Freedom: Sweet Honey in the Rock . . . Still on the Journey* (Anchor Books, 1993), and *Voices of the Civil Rights Movement, Black American Freedom Songs* (Smithsonian/Folkways Recordings, 1980, 1994) a 2-CD anthology. Reagon has served as music consultant, composer, and performer for several radio, film, and video projects, including the path-breaking, Peabody Award–winning 1994 radio series *Wade in the Water: African-American Sacred Music Traditions* (produced by National Public Radio and the Smithsonian Institution); composer, compiler, and performer in the creation of the sound scores for WGBH's Peabody Award-winning *Africans in America* film series for PBS (1998); and *Freedom Never Dies: The Legacy of Harry T. Moore* (The Documentary Institute at the University of Florida and WUFT-TV, 2001).

WHOLE WHEAT ROLLS

½	cup table cream	1	package dry yeast
½	cup milk	1	egg, well beaten
¼	cup + 1 tablespoon sugar, divided	2	cups whole wheat flour
¾	teaspoon salt	1½	cups all-purpose flour
¼	cup shortening		Melted unsalted butter
¼	cup warm water	¼	cup melted unsalted butter
		2	teaspoons honey

Combine cream and milk, heat until scalding, and stir in ¼ cup of the sugar, salt, and shortening. Stir until shortening melts, and cool to lukewarm. While milk mixture is cooling, place warm water in a separate bowl, sprinkle yeast on water surface. Next, add 1 tablespoon of sugar. Stir mixture until sugar dissolves. Allow yeast to "proof" before adding it to the milk mixture. (*Proofing* is simply the means by which the yeast is proved to be good. Fresh yeast will foam, as opposed to dead yeast, which lies flat in the water.) Add egg and whole wheat flour, beat well until batter is smooth. Add all-purpose flour and lightly knead to form a smooth dough. Place in a greased bowl and turn to grease top. Cover with a tea towel and allow to rise 1½ to 2 hours or until doubled in bulk. Punch dough down, divide into two equal parts. Turn half of the dough out onto a floured surface and roll into a circle 10 inches in diameter and ¼ inch thick. Brush with butter. Cut circle into 12 equal wedges. Roll each wedge tightly toward the tip. Seal points and place on a lightly greased baking sheet with the tip underneath. Curve into a crescent shape. Repeat process with remaining dough and set rolls aside to rise until doubled in bulk, approximately 1 hour. Bake for approximately 10 minutes or until golden brown. Combine ¼ cup butter and honey and lightly brush each crescent with mixture.

Approximately 2 dozen crescent rolls

Ossie Davis

The profoundest commitment possible to a black creator in this country today—
beyond all creeds, crafts, classes, and ideologies whatsoever—is to bring before
his people the scent of freedom.

—Ossie Davis

This tall and dignified actor with a magnificent stage voice was born the son of a railroad engineer on December 18, 1917, in Cogdell, Georgia. As a young man, he set out on foot from Waycross, Georgia, to attend Howard University. Against the advice of his professor, Alain Locke, he left Howard in 1939, prior to graduating, and moved to New York to join Harlem's Rose McClendon players. (On May 12, 1973, he was awarded a doctor of humanities degree by Howard University.)

After serving in the army during World War II, Davis returned to New York, where he made his 1946 Broadway debut in the title role of *Jeb*, a play by Robert Ardrey. He also met his future wife, Ruby Dee. Numerous Broadway roles followed, including the lead in *A Raisin in the Sun*. In 1960 he had perhaps his biggest hit when he wrote and starred in the critically acclaimed *Purlie Victorious*, a play that was later adapted for the screen and for the Broadway musical *Purlie*.

Davis made his film debut with Sidney Poitier in *No Way Out* in 1950. Subsequent film credits included *The Cardinal* (1963), *A Man Called Adam* (1966), and *Slaves* (1969), among others. As popular today as ever, he has recently appeared in *School Daze* (1988), *Do the Right Thing* (1989), *Jungle Fever* (1991), *Grumpy Old Men* (1993), and *The Client* (1995).

Davis made his directorial debut in 1970 with an adaptation of the Chester Himes novel *Cotton Comes to Harlem*. Additional directorial credits include: *Kongi's Harvest* (1971), *Black Girl* (1972), *Gordon's War* (1973), and *Countdown at Kusini* (1976).

He first appeared on television in a 1951 production of *Green Pastures*, followed by appearances in *Roots: The Next Generations*, *Evening Shade*, *The Stand*, and *The Promised Land*.

Politically active and highly visible during the civil rights movement, Davis raised money for the Freedom Riders and eulogized both Malcolm X and Martin Luther King, Jr. Named to the NAACP Image Awards Hall of Fame with wife Ruby Dee in 1989, he and Dee were celebrated as National Treasures when they received the National Medal of Arts in 1995. In 2000, they received the Life Achievement Award from the Screen Actors Guild of America.

CLOVER LEAF POTATO ROLLS

1	package dry yeast	¾	teaspoon salt
½	cup warm water	⅔	cup soft butter
½	cup sugar	½	cup milk
1	cup cold mashed potatoes	½	cup half-and-half
2	eggs, well beaten		Up to 6 cups all-purpose flour

Proof yeast (see p. 226) in warm water with half of the sugar. Mix together potatoes, remaining sugar, eggs, salt, and butter and set aside. Combine milk and half-and-half in a double boiler, stir and scald the milk mixture before adding it to the potato mixture. Stir in yeast mixture and sufficient flour to make a stiff dough. Place in greased bowl and cover, and allow to rise until doubled in size. (At this point the bread dough can be refrigerated and stored up to 4 days.) Punch down dough and knead slightly. Shape into clover rolls by rolling dough into ¾- to 1-inch balls. Place three balls into each tin of a cupcake tin. They should fill the bottom of tin without overcrowding. Allow rolls to rise until doubled in size and bake for 8 minutes in a preheated 400°F oven.

3 to 4 dozen rolls

YEAST BISCUITS

4	cups sifted flour	1	package dry yeast
2	tablespoons granulated sugar	3	tablespoons warm water
3	teaspoons baking powder	¼	teaspoon sugar
1	teaspoon baking soda	2	cups buttermilk
1	teaspoon salt		Melted butter
1	cup chilled shortening		

Preheat oven to 400°F. Lightly butter a baking sheet and set aside. Sift together dry ingredients and cut in the chilled shortening until the mixture resembles coarse corn meal. Proof the yeast (see p. 226) in warm water to which ¼ teaspoon of sugar has been added. Combine yeast mixture with buttermilk and add to the dry ingredients. Mix well and turn dough out onto a lightly floured surface. The dough will be sticky; however, add additional flour in small amounts as necessary to facilitate handling. Roll dough to a thickness of ½ inch and cut with a biscuit cutter. Dip each biscuit in melted butter, place on a baking sheet, and bake for 15 to 20 minutes.

12 to 14 biscuits

BAKING POWDER BISCUITS

2	cups unsifted flour	¾ teaspoon salt
1	teaspoon baking powder	¼ cup shortening
1	tablespoon sugar	Up to ¾ cup milk

Preheat oven to 450°F. In a large mixing bowl, sift together dry ingredients; cut in shortening until mixture resembles coarse corn meal, then slowly add milk to the flour mixture. Use only enough of the milk to hold the flour mixture together. Turn out onto a floured surface and roll to a thickness of ½ inch. Cut with a biscuit cutter and bake in a preheated oven for 10 to 12 minutes.

10 to 12 biscuits

Dr. Debbie Allen

One lesson that Debbie Allen took to heart and brought to her role as Lydia Grant in the movie *Fame* is that fame costs. A multitalented artist, she started paying sweat equity at age three when she began dance lessons. Although Allen was rejected by the Houston Ballet School, her mother, a Pulitzer Prize–nominated poet, encouraged her 12-year-old daughter to pursue her dream of a career in dancing. Allen took private lessons with a former dancer from the Ballets Russes, moved to Mexico City, and got a job with the Ballet Nacional de Mexico. Upon returning to Houston in 1964, she reauditioned for the Houston Foundation for Ballet, and this time her "never give up" attitude paid off. She received a full scholarship and was the company's first black dancer. Allen went on to attend Howard, graduating with honors in 1971, then pursued a Broadway career. She appeared in *Purlie* (a musical version of Ossie Davis's *Purlie Victorious*) and in *Raisin,* and her big theatrical break came in 1980, when she played Anita in *West Side Story* and was honored with a Drama Desk Award and a Tony nomination. This success was followed by a role in the 1980 hit movie *Fame,* and Allen also starred in the television spinoff, earning two Emmys and a Golden Globe during the show's five-year run. She received a second Tony nomination in 1986 for her role in Bob Fosse's *Sweet Charity.*

Allen has directed several episodes of *Fame,* produced and directed *The Cosby Show* spinoff *A Different World,* and directed episodes of *The Fresh Prince of Bel-Air, Quantum Leap,* and a Martin Luther King special entitled *One Day* for the Disney Channel. She choreographed the Academy Awards show from 1991 to 1994, and has written the children's books *Brothers of the Knight* and *Dancing in the Wings.*

Debbie Allen was awarded an honorary doctorate from Howard University in 1992, won the Essence Award in 1992, and the first Lena Horne Award for Career Achievement in 1995. She continues to produce, direct, and act, and she runs her own dance academy in Los Angeles.

QUICK BISCUIT MIX

8 cups flour
1½ cups nonfat dry milk
5 tablespoons double-acting
    baking powder

1 tablespoon salt
1 cup chilled shortening

In a large mixing bowl, combine dry ingredients and mix well to combine. Work in shortening with fingertips until mixture resembles fine meal. Store mix in refrigerator until ready to use. (Yields approximately 10 cups of quick biscuit mix.)

To make 18 biscuits, add ¾ cup water to 2¾ cups of the biscuit mixture, stir, and add a few additional tablespoons of water, one tablespoon at a time, to form a soft dough. Turn mixture out onto a lightly floured surface and knead lightly. Cut into 2-inch rounds, place on a baking sheet, and bake in a preheated 425° F oven for 10 to 12 minutes.

18 biscuits

LIBERIAN RICE BREAD

1 cup rice meal or cream
    of wheat
1 teaspoon baking powder
⅛ teaspoon baking soda
¼ cup sugar
¼ teaspoon nutmeg
    Pinch allspice

¼ teaspoon salt
¾ cup mashed plantain or banana
    (under-ripe)
½ teaspoon vanilla extract
¾ cup milk
1 egg, well beaten
¼ cup melted butter

Preheat oven to 350°F. Butter an 8 × 12-inch baking dish and set aside. In a large bowl, combine the dry ingredients and set aside. In a separate bowl, combine mashed plantain or banana with remaining ingredients and mix well before adding to the dry ingredients and mixing well. Pour into baking dish and bake in a preheated oven for approximately 1 hour.

6 to 8 servings

WHOLE WHEAT ZUCCHINI BREAD

¾ cup whole wheat flour
¾ cup all-purpose flour
1½ teaspoons baking powder
½ teaspoon baking soda
1¼ teaspoons ground cinnamon
¾ teaspoon ground nutmeg
1 egg, well beaten

¼ cup sugar
2 teaspoons vanilla
2 tablespoons butter, melted
1½ cups finely shredded, unpeeled zucchini
¾ cups golden raisins

Butter a 4 × 8–inch loaf pan and set aside. Preheat oven to 350°F. Combine flours, baking powder, baking soda, and spices, and mix well. In a separate bowl, combine egg, sugar, vanilla, and butter; mix until well blended. Add zucchini and raisins. Gradually add the mixture to the dry ingredients and mix until moistened. Pour into loaf pan and bake 50 minutes, or until a tester comes out clean. Cool in pan 10 minutes, and then turn out onto rack to finish cooling.

8 to 10 servings

Phylicia Rashad

Phylicia Ayers-Allen was born in Houston, Texas, graduated magnum cum laude from Howard University and went to New York City to pursue a career on stage. She won roles in *Into the Woods, The Cherry Orchard,* and *Weep not for Me* and appeared often on television, where her best-known role is probably that of Claire Huxtable, a successful no-nonsense attorney and loving mother, playing opposite television husband Bill Cosby.

A member of Howard University's Board of Trustees, she is also a member of Alpha Kappa Alpha sorority and a committed supporter of numerous charitable and educational organizations, including the Diabetes Association African-American Program and the Educational Teacher's Association.

She has won an NAACP Image Award for Best Actress in a Comedy Series, and as an accomplished and versatile singer, she performs as a guest soloist with major symphonies across the United States.

OLD-FASHIONED LOAF BREAD

Nothing says "I love you" like the fragrance of freshly baked bread. Show your love in a special way with this old-fashioned loaf bread recipe.

¼ cup warm water (110 to 115°F)	2 tablespoons sugar
¼ teaspoon sugar	2 teaspoons salt
1 package active dry yeast	1 tablespoon shortening
2 cups milk	Up to 6 cups sifted all-purpose flour

Grease two 9¼ × 5¼ × 2¾-inch loaf pans and set aside. Combine warm water and sugar and mix well. Proof yeast (see p. 226) in warm water mixture. Scald milk and add 2 tablespoons of sugar, salt, and shortening. Allow mixture to cool to lukewarm. Add 2 cups of flour, stirring well. Add proofed yeast and sufficient additional flour to form a moderately stiff dough. Turn dough out onto a lightly floured surface and knead until the dough is smooth and satiny. Roll dough into a ball and place in a lightly greased bowl. Turn dough to grease top. Cover the bowl and allow the dough to rise until it doubles in size, approximately 1½ hours. Punch down dough and divide into 2 equal parts, shape into 2 loaves. Place in prepared pans and allow to rise until doubled, approximately 1 hour. Bake in a preheated 400°F oven for 50 minutes.

Yields 2 loaves

BLACK-EYED PEA CORNBREAD

1 cup corn meal	2 eggs, well beaten
½ cup flour	1 cup buttermilk
½ teaspoon salt	¾ cup corn, drained
½ teaspoon baking soda	1 cup cooked black-eyed peas
½ teaspoon baking powder	1 pound fried bacon, crumbled
½ cup vegetable oil	

Preheat oven to 350°F. Lightly butter an 11 × 14-inch baking pan and set aside. Combine corn meal, flour, salt, baking soda, baking powder, vegetable oil, eggs, and buttermilk; mix well. Stir in corn, black-eyed peas, and bacon. Pour into prepared baking pan and bake in a preheated oven for 30 to 35 minutes until golden brown and a tester inserted into the center comes out clean.

12 servings

HONEY CORNBREAD

It will melt in your mouth and have you asking for seconds before you have finished your first piece! Better make two pans.

¾ cup all-purpose flour	½ cup heavy cream
1 cup yellow corn meal	½ cup half-and-half
1 tablespoon baking powder	¼ cup melted butter
2 tablespoons granulated sugar	¼ cup honey
¼ teaspoon nutmeg	2 eggs, well beaten

Preheat oven to 400°F. Lightly butter a 9 × 9-inch square baking pan and set aside. In a large bowl, combine the flour, corn meal, baking powder, sugar, and nutmeg and stir to blend. In a separate bowl, combine heavy cream, half-and-half, butter, and honey, mix well. Add eggs and mix to blend. Add cream mixture to the dry ingredients and stir to combine. Pour into prepared pan and bake in preheated oven for 20 to 25 minutes until golden brown and a tester inserted in the center comes out clean.

8 servings

Jessye Norman

She had all of the tools—she was very intelligent, a keen musician, and a voice with
qualities you encounter a few times in a generation. I've never heard another like
her in all my years at [the University of Michigan] . . . Jessye has a special ability
to absorb the flavor and accents of the languages in the country where she performs.
She functions like a linguist as well as a singer . . . She is a fine, complete musician.
She can talk about and understand compositions and composers.
That's not something all singers can do.

—Willis Patterson,
Associate Dean and Professor of Music, University of Michigan

Jessye Norman hails from Augusta, Georgia, one of five children born into the loving and musical family of Silas Norman, an insurance broker who sang at church, and Janie Norman, an amateur pianist who encouraged all of her children to take piano lessons and sing. Jessye took to her lessons with zeal, singing at school, Girl Scout meetings, and reportedly, once at a supermarket opening. Her musical passion was opera, which she recalls falling in love with at age nine while listening to a broadcast of the Metropolitan Opera.

When she was sixteen Jessye's high school choir director accompanied her to Philadelphia where she competed in the Marion Anderson Scholarship Contest. Although she did not win the scholarship, on the way home they visited the music department at Howard University, where Jessye sang for faculty member Carolyn Grant and received an immediate recommendation for a full scholarship. Jessye Norman graduated magna cum laude from Howard University in 1967 with a bachelor's in music and went on to take a master's at the University of Michigan School of Music.

She soon won the International Music Competition in Munich, and a host of European singing offers followed. At age 23, she debuted with the Deutsche Opera in Berlin, and since then she has sung to wide acclaim in most of Europe's major opera houses and concert halls.

She made her U.S. debut at the Hollywood Bowl in 1972, and has performed starring roles on every important opera stage in this country, too. Norman has received honorary doctorates from dozens of colleges, universities, and conservatories. In 1989, she was awarded the Legion d'Honneur by French President Francois Mitterrand, and in 1990, she was named honorary ambassador to the United Nations by U.N. Secretary General Xavier Perez de Cuellar. Among her numerous awards are multiple Grammys, an Ace Award, and the Paris Grand Prix National du Disque.

In addition to performing, Norman serves on the boards of directors for the Ms. Foundation, the National Music Foundation, City-Meals-on-Wheels in New York City, and the New York Botanical Garden. She is also the national spokesperson for the Partnership for the Homeless and the Lupus Foundation, and is a member of the board of trustees of Paine College in Augusta, Georgia.

J.R.'s Skillet Cornbread

½	cup all-purpose flour	¼	teaspoon salt
1	cup yellow corn meal	1	cup whole milk
¼	cup sugar	1	egg, beaten
1½	teaspoons baking powder	¼	cup vegetable oil

Preheat the oven to 425°F. Mix dry ingredients in a large bowl. Slowly add the milk, beaten egg, and vegetable oil, and mix well; set aside. Pour the oil into a 10-inch cast-iron skillet, and place it in the preheated oven for approximately 10 minutes. (Oil should start to smoke.) Remove the skillet from the oven and carefully pour the batter into it. Reduce oven temperature to 400°F and bake for 20 to 25 minutes. Remove bread from the oven and brown under a broiler, if necessary. Turn cornbread out onto an ovenproof plate and serve hot with butter.

8 servings

CREAMED-CORN CORNBREAD

1	tablespoon vegetable oil		1	cup half-and-half
2	cups yellow corn meal		2	eggs
1	teaspoon salt		1	cup cream-style corn
2	teaspoons granulated sugar			Pinch of nutmeg
2½	teaspoons baking powder			

Preheat oven to 425°F. Place vegetable oil in the skillet and place skillet in the oven to heat for a few minutes. Meanwhile, combine the corn meal, salt, sugar, and baking powder in a bowl, and mix to combine.

In a separate bowl, combine the half-and-half, eggs, corn, and nutmeg, stirring until well blended. Combine the dry and liquid ingredients and mix well. If the batter is too stiff to pour, add additional cream, a small amount at a time. Pour the batter into the heated skillet and bake in the preheated oven, approximately 20 minutes or until the cornbread is golden brown.

8 servings

Roberta Flack and Donny Hathaway

The outstanding musical duo of Roberta Flack and Donny Hathaway met and became friends at Howard University. They have since created a lasting musical legacy, composed of collaborative hits such as *The Closer I Get to You, Where Is the Love, You Are My Heaven,* and *Back Together Again.* Both pursued individual careers as well; Hathaway behind the scenes as a producer, arranger, songwriter, and session pianist/keyboardist working with music legends such as Aretha Franklin, Stevie Wonder, Jerry Butler, the Staples Singers, and Curtis Mayfield, and Flack as a teacher and solo performer. Roberta Flack's most popular song is no doubt the chartbusting success "First Time Ever I Saw Your Face," recorded in 1969. Two other hits, "Feel Like Making Love," and "Killing Me Softly with His Song" quickly followed. After Hathaway's tragic death in 1979, Flack partnered with Peabo Bryson to produce the commercially successful hit "I Celebrate My Love," and with Maxi Priest for "Set the Night to Music."

THYME CORN STICKS

Excellent with a hearty stew or soup!

1¼	cups corn meal	1	teaspoon dried thyme
¾	cup flour	2	large eggs, lightly beaten
1	tablespoon sugar	1	cup buttermilk
1	tablespoon baking powder	¼	cup vegetable oil
1	teaspoon onion powder		

Grease cast-iron corn stick pans and place into a preheated 425°F oven. Combine dry ingredients and mix well. In a separate bowl, combine the eggs, buttermilk, and vegetable oil. Mix well and stir into the dry ingredients until just combined. Remove pans from the oven and spoon the batter into them, filling ⅔ full. Return pans to the preheated oven and bake 12 minutes or until the corn sticks are golden.

18 servings

HUSH PUPPIES

1	egg	2	teaspoons salt
2	cups buttermilk	¼	teaspoon onion powder
2	cups yellow corn meal	⅛	teaspoon cayenne pepper
1½	teaspoons baking soda	2	tablespoons all-purpose flour
1	tablespoon baking powder	⅓	cup onion, chopped

Combine egg and buttermilk, mix well, and set aside. In a separate bowl, thoroughly combine the dry ingredients. Add chopped onion and stir until onion is thoroughly dispersed throughout the corn meal mixture, and blend in buttermilk mixture. Fill cast iron skillet with vegetable oil to a depth of 1½ inches and heat to 370°F. Shape hush puppies, drop into the hot oil, and fry until evenly browned. Drain on paper towels and serve immediately.

12 to 14 servings

DESSERTS

Dr. Polly Quick Brown

Following the decision in *Brown*, Polly Quick integrated Bancroft Elementary School in Washington, D.C. After receiving undergraduate and graduate degrees from Howard University, where she met her future husband, Nathan Brown, she entered the University of Minnesota in 1978, becoming its first black female Ph.D. Today Polly is the principal of Thaddeus Stevens Elementary School. Founded for freed slaves in 1868, it is the oldest school of its kind in Washington, D.C. *(Private collection)*

PINTO BEAN PIE

4	eggs, beaten	2	teaspoons vanilla extract
2	cups sugar	⅛	teaspoon cinnamon
1½	cup cooked, unseasoned pinto beans, drained and mashed	1½	sticks butter, melted
		2	8-inch unbaked pie shells

Preheat oven to 450°F. Beat eggs until they are foamy. Add sugar and continue to beat until well blended. Add beans, vanilla, and cinnamon; continue beating mixture until it is smooth. Pour mixture into pie shells and bake in preheated oven for 30 to 35 minutes or until a tester inserted into the pie's center comes out clean.

8 servings

BUTTERMILK PIE

1½	cups sugar	¾	cup buttermilk
2	eggs, well beaten	2¼	teaspoons vanilla
2	tablespoons flour		Pinch of nutmeg
1	stick butter (8 tablespoons)	1	9-inch unbaked pie shell

Preheat oven to 450°F. Combine the first 7 ingredients, mix well, and pour into pie shell. Bake until custard begins to brown, approximately 25 minutes. Reduce heat to 200°F and bake until custard sets, approximately 20 minutes.

6 to 8 servings

Herbert O. Reid

Revered by hundreds of HU graduates, Professor Reid was among the first, if not the first African-American to clerk at the state supreme court level. Herbert Odré Reid, Sr., introduced the Houston tradition of jurisprudence to students in Legal Method and Constitutional Law and challenged them to live up to the highest standards of social responsibility. During the more than forty years that he taught at the law school, he instructed generations of lawyers to think and act as social engineers, to make the world a better place than it was before they started practicing.

Reid filed an amicus brief in *Bakke,* a landmark reverse discrimination case, that Justice Thurgood Marshall named the "best brief" the Court had received. When students were arrested for protesting in segregated Alabama, Reid went before the state's appellate courts to argue for their freedom-of-speech rights. He fought in southern states for equal funding of historically black colleges and universities. Never one to shy from any tough fight, he investigated the 1969 killing of Black Panther Party members by federal law enforcement officers in Chicago. And when Adam Clayton Powell was denied his seat in Congress, Reid was among the team of attorneys who argued before the courts that Congress lacked the authority to do so.

Professor Reid's lifelong commitment to civil and human rights was recognized in 1979 when he was awarded the prestigious Charles Hamilton Houston Medallion of Merit by the Washington Bar Association.

VANILLA CREAM PIE

1 cup sugar	3 tablespoons butter, divided
½ cup flour	2 teaspoons vanilla extract
Dash of salt	1 9-inch baked pie shell
3 cups half-and-half	Whipped cream
4 egg yolks, beaten	

Preheat oven to 350°F. Combine sugar, flour, and salt in a saucepan. Gradually stir in half-and-half and cook over medium-high heat until thickened mixture bubbles. Continue to cook for an additional minute, stirring to prevent scorching. In a small heatproof bowl, combine hot mixture and egg yolks, stir until well blended. Return egg yolk mixture to saucepan. Bring to a gentle boil and stir while cooking an additional 2 minutes. Remove from heat. Stir butter and vanilla extract into the mixture and pour into baked pie shell. Bake for 12 to 15 minutes until shell is golden, cool, cover, and refrigerate until it is served. Garnish with whipped cream just before serving.

8 servings

CHOCOLATE CREAM PIE

1¼ cups sugar	4 egg yolks, beaten
½ cup flour	3 tablespoons butter, divided
Dash of salt	2 teaspoons vanilla extract
3 cups half-and-half	1 9-inch baked pie shell
3 squares (3 ounces) unsweetened chocolate	Chocolate shavings and whipped cream for topping

Preheat oven to 350°F. Combine sugar, flour, and salt in a saucepan. Gradually stir in half-and-half and cook over medium-high heat until thickened mixture bubbles. Add chocolate and stir until it melts. Continue cooking mixture for an additional minute, stirring to prevent scorching. In a small heatproof bowl, combine hot mixture and egg yolks, stir until well-blended. Return egg yolk mixture to saucepan. Bring to a gentle boil and stir while cooking an additional 2 minutes. Remove from heat. Stir butter and vanilla extract into the mixture and pour into baked pie shell. Bake for 12 to 15 minutes until shell is golden, cool, cover and refrigerate until it is served. Top with whipped cream and chocolate shavings just before serving.

8 servings

CHOCOLATE PECAN PIE

3   eggs, beaten
1   square unsweetened chocolate
3   tablespoons butter
¾   cup sugar
1   cup Karo syrup

2   teaspoons vanilla
1¼   cups pecans, finely chopped
1   9-inch unbaked pie shell
     Whipped cream

Beat eggs in a large, heatproof bowl and set aside. Melt chocolate and butter in a double boiler. In a separate saucepan, combine sugar and syrup, bring to a rapid boil, reduce heat, and continue to boil slowly for an additional 2 minutes. Add chocolate mixture, mix well, and pour slowly over eggs, stirring constantly. Add vanilla and pecans. Mix well. Pour into an unbaked pie shell and bake at 375°F for 45 minutes until a tester inserted into the pie's center comes out clean. Cool and garnish with whipped cream before serving.

8 servings

SWEET POTATO PECAN PIE

4	eggs	⅛	teaspoon salt
1½	cups boiled sweet potatoes, mashed	1	9-inch unbaked pie shell
⅓	cup sugar	½	cup heavy cream
½	cup pecans, finely chopped	⅛	teaspoon ground nutmeg
1	cup orange juice	⅛	teaspoon cinnamon
2	teaspoons vanilla extract	1	tablespoon grated orange zest

Preheat oven to 450°F. Beat eggs until they are light and frothy. Add sweet potatoes, sugar, pecans, orange juice, vanilla, and salt, beating well after each addition. Pour into pie shell and bake 10 minutes. Reduce temperature to 350°F and bake 30 additional minutes or until the crust is golden brown and a tester inserted into the pie's center comes out clean. Place on a rack to cool. Next, whip heavy cream until stiff peaks form, add nutmeg and cinnamon. Place a dollop of whipped cream mixture on each individual serving of pie and garnish with orange zest.

6 to 8 servings

WHITE POTATO PIE

1	cup granulated sugar	1	cup half-and-half
½	teaspoon baking powder	2	tablespoons lemon juice
⅛	teaspoon salt	1	teaspoon vanilla extract
2	large baking potatoes, peeled, boiled, and mashed	4	eggs, beaten
⅔	cup butter	¼	teaspoon nutmeg
		2	9-inch unbaked pie shells

Preheat oven to 350°F. Combine sugar, baking powder, and salt, add potatoes, and mix well. Add butter and continue to mix until well blended. Gradually add half-and-half and remaining ingredients and mix well. Spoon mixture into pie shells and bake for 55 minutes or until a tester inserted into the center comes out clean. Cool before serving.

5 to 8 servings

STRAWBERRY BANANA PIE

1   quart strawberries
¾   cup sugar
2½   tablespoons strawberry
        gelatin
1   cup water

Pinch of salt
3   bananas, peeled and sliced
1   9-inch baked pie shell
Whipped cream

Clean and hull strawberries. Place 1 cup of the strawberries in a saucepan with sugar, gelatin, water, and salt. Cook mixture over medium-high heat until it is slightly thickened. Next, combine bananas and remaining strawberries and pour into pie shell, mounding high in the middle. Pour syrup over the mixture and chill for at least 4 hours before serving. Garnish with fresh whipped cream.

6 to 8 servings

CHERRY CRUMB PIE

1   9-inch unbaked pie shell
1   can cherries, drained (reserve
        juice)
1   cup sugar
2   tablespoons cornstarch

½   tablespoon butter
½   tablespoon lemon juice
¼   teaspoon almond extract
3   drops red food coloring (optional)

Preheat oven to 375°F. Combine sugar and half of the cherry juice; cook until sugar dissolves. Combine cornstarch and remaining cherry juice. Reduce heat to medium and continue to cook until mixture thickens. Next, add cherries, butter, and remaining ingredients. Pour mixture into pie shell and top with crumb topping (see recipe below). Bake for approximately 45 minutes, or until the crumb topping browns.

6 to 8 servings

CRUMB TOPPING

1 cup unsifted flour	¼ cup softened butter
½ cup light brown sugar	

Combine ingredients in a small bowl and rub together with your fingertips until the mixture resembles coarse meal.

James Adali Cobb

James Adali Cobb, born in 1876 on a Shreveport, Louisiana, plantation, endured a harsh boyhood and was orphaned by age eight. Determined to improve himself, he found his way into a private school and eventually to Straight University (now Dillard). He earned his law degree from Howard University in 1899, a master of law degree in 1901, and a Pd.B. in 1902.

In 1907, he was named a special assistant with the United States Department of Justice, one of the first African-Americans to hold that position. He was soon assigned to the office of the United States attorney, where he was the first African-American assistant U.S. attorney. As the clouds of World War I were gathering in 1916, Cobbs joined the faculty at Howard University Law School, where he taught a variety of courses, including constitutional law. He also maintained an influential African-American law practice, hiring talented black lawyers who, at the time, would not have been hired by any other Washington, D.C., firm. The Moot Court room at Howard is named in his honor.

APPLE, RAISIN, AND WALNUT PIE

Pie dough sufficient for a
  2-crust pie
2   tablespoons all-purpose flour
¾   cup granulated sugar
½   teaspoon cinnamon
⅛   teaspoon ground nutmeg

Pinch allspice
5   cups apples, peeled, cored and
      coarsely chopped
¾   cup raisins
½   cup coarsely chopped walnuts

Preheat oven to 375°F. Prepare pie dough and place crust in 9-inch pie pan; reserve remainder of dough for the top crust. Combine the flour, sugar, cinnamon, nutmeg, and allspice and set aside. Combine apples, raisins, and walnuts in a large bowl and gently combine with the sugar mixture until well mixed. Pour into pie shell. Top with crust and vent to allow steam to escape. Bake in a preheated oven for 40 to 50 minutes, or until filling is set and the crust is golden brown.

16 servings

PIE GLAZE

1   cup sifted confectioner's
      sugar
¼   teaspoon vanilla extract

2   tablespoons light cream

Combine the above ingredients, mix well, and drizzle over cooled pies.

COCONUT PECAN RAISIN PIE

½   cup melted butter
2   eggs
½   cup coarsely chopped pecans
1   tablespoon white vinegar
1   cup sugar

¼   teaspoon ground cinnamon
¼   cup flaked coconut
¼   cup seedless raisins
1   unbaked 8-inch pie shell

Preheat oven to 300°F. Combine the first 8 ingredients and pour into pie shell. Bake for one hour and fifteen minutes or until tester inserted in pie's center comes out clean.

6 to 8 servings

*(Photograph courtesy
Howard University Archives)*

Kelly Miller

Kelly Miller was the sixth of ten children born to Kelly Miller, Sr., a free Negro, and Elizabeth Roberts Miller, a slave. His earliest teachers had come south after the end of the civil war to teach the freedmen, and he later lovingly referred to them as "a band of heroes . . . who sowed the seed of intelligence in the soil of ignorance."

In 1880 Miller entered the preparatory department of Howard University as a scholarship student and he received his bachelor of science from Howard University in 1886. In 1887 upon the recommendation of noted astronomer Simon Newcombe, Miller became the first African-American graduate student and the first African-American student to be admitted to Johns Hopkins University. He was appointed professor of mathematics at Howard in 1890, introduced sociology into Howard's curriculum in 1895. From 1895 to 1907, he served as professor of mathematics and sociology; he was also appointed dean of the College of Arts and Sciences.

The prolific Miller wrote several books on a variety of subjects, and his articles appeared often in the major periodicals of the day; at one time his weekly column appeared in more than 100 newspapers. A tireless spokesperson for the value of African-American education, he spent many summers touring the country to encourage African-American children in their pursuit of learning. He was the father of five outstanding and successful children.

PEANUT BUTTER PIE

I know. I, too, was skeptical at first—and then I tasted it, and all my childhood confectionary fantasies came true!

½	cup chunky peanut butter	1	cup confectioner's sugar
1	8-ounce package cream cheese, softened	8	ounces Cool Whip
		1	graham cracker pie crust
½	cup table cream	½	cup miniature chocolate chips

Use a hand mixer to cream together peanut butter, cream cheese, table cream, and sugar. Fold Cool Whip into this mixture and blend. Place blended mixture into pie crust and freeze one hour. Allow to set at room temperature and sprinkle with chocolate chips before serving.

8 servings

PINTO BEAN CAKE

1	stick (8 tablespoons) butter, softened	½	teaspoon salt
1	cup sugar	1¼	teaspoons cinnamon
2	cups cooked and unseasoned pinto beans, well mashed	1	teaspoon allspice
			Pinch of ground cloves
1	tablespoon vanilla extract	½	cup chopped pecans
2	eggs	1	cup yellow raisins
1	cup all-purpose flour	2	cups Granny Smith apples, peeled and finely chopped
1	teaspoon baking soda		

Preheat oven to 325°F. Grease and flour a 10-inch tube pan and set aside. Cream butter with an electric mixer until it is light and fluffy. Gradually add sugar while continuing to beat. Add beans and blend well. Stir in remaining ingredients. Mix well. Pour into a prepared pan and bake in preheated oven for 1 hour.

8 to 10 servings

COCONUT POUND CAKE

6 eggs, separated (reserve
   whites)
½ cup shortening
1 cup butter
3 cups baker's sugar

1 teaspoon vanilla extract
3 cups sifted cake flour
1 cup low-fat buttermilk
1 3½-ounce can flaked coconut
Powdered sugar

Separate the eggs and allow whites to warm to room temperature. Preheat oven to 300°F. Grease and flour a 10-inch tube pan and set aside. Using a mixer at high speed, cream together shortening and butter. Gradually add sugar and extract; beat until well blended. Reduce speed to low and gradually add flour and buttermilk, ¼ cup at a time. Add coconut; beat until well blended. Beat egg whites until stiff peaks form. Gently fold whites into batter until well mixed. Turn into the prepared pan. Bake 2 hours or until cake tester inserted into the center comes out clean. Remove from pan to a wire rack to cool. When still slightly warm, dust cake with powdered sugar.

10 to 12 servings

SOUR CREAM AND LEMON-THYME POUND CAKE

2¾ cups all-purpose flour
3 tablespoons fresh thyme,
   chopped
½ teaspoon baking soda
¾ teaspoon cinnamon
⅛ teaspoon nutmeg
¼ teaspoon salt

1 cup unsalted butter, softened
2 cups baker's sugar
2 teaspoons lemon extract
6 eggs, room temperature
1 cup sour cream
¼ cup fresh lemon juice

Preheat oven to 350°F. Grease and flour a 10-inch bundt pan and set aside. Combine flour, thyme, baking soda, cinnamon, nutmeg, and salt; mix well and set aside. In a separate bowl, beat butter until it is fluffy, gradually add sugar and continue to beat until fluffy. Add lemon extract and beat an additional 3 minutes. Beat in eggs one at a time, beating well after each addition. Combine sour cream and lemon juice, mix well to blend. Add sour cream mixture to flour mixture in three additions, beat well after each addition. Pour into bundt pan and bake in preheated oven for 55 minutes or until a tester inserted in the cake's center comes out clean. Remove from pan and cool 15 minutes before brushing with glaze.

8 to 10 servings

GLAZE

½ cup lemon juice	2 teaspoons lemon zest
½ cup baker's sugar	Thin lemon slices
1 tablespoon minced fresh thyme	Fresh raspberries

Combine lemon juice, sugar, and thyme and cook over medium-high heat until sugar dissolves. Bring mixture to a boil and continue to boil until mixture thickens and becomes syrupy, approximately 10 minutes. Cool 5 minutes and brush over cooled cake. Garnish with lemon slices and fresh raspberries.

CHOCOLATE POUND CAKE

2 sticks butter (½ pound)	3 cups all-purpose flour
½ cup shortening	½ teaspoon salt
5 eggs	1 cup evaporated milk
3 cups granulated sugar	2½ teaspoons vanilla extract
½ cup cocoa	Pinch of cinnamon
½ teaspoon baking powder	1 cup pecan halves

Preheat oven to 325°F. Grease and flour a bundt cake pan and set aside. Cream together the butter and shortening. Add the eggs, one at a time, beating well after each addition. In a separate bowl, sift together all of the dry ingredients, including the cocoa. Combine the milk, vanilla extract, and cinnamon, and set aside. Add dry ingredients to butter mixture, a cup at a time, beating well after each addition; alternate with addition of milk mixture. Pour batter into the prepared bundt pan, sprinkle evenly with the nuts, and bake in preheated oven for 1 hour or until a tester inserted in the cake's center comes out clean.

7 servings

John Mercer Langston

Uncle of acclaimed poet Langston Hughes, John Mercer Langston was born free in 1829 in Louisa County, Virginia, the youngest of four children of Ralph Quarles, a wealthy white planter and slaveholder. His mother, Lucy Langston, was an emancipated slave of Native-American and black ancestry.

Following the death of his parents Langston received an inheritance that left him financially independent. At age fourteen, he enrolled in the Preparatory Department at Oberlin College, where he excelled at debate and he became involved in the black rights movement. In 1848, he was invited by Frederick Douglass to deliver an impromptu speech to the National Black Convention in Cleveland, condemning those who refused to help fugitive slaves.

Although Langston obtained a master's degree in theology from Oberlin, his application to the law school was rejected. Langston read law under an attorney instead, passing the bar in 1854 to become the first black lawyer in Ohio. His commitment to black freedom continued to grow, and together with his brothers Gideon and Charles, Langston organized antislavery societies and assisted slaves in their escape along the Ohio section of the Underground Railroad.

After Langston married Caroline Wall, they settled in Brownhelm, Ohio, and he established a law practice there. In 1855, he was elected town clerk, and, though not yet verified, it is believed that he was the first African-American elected to public office in the United States.

Langston returned to Oberlin in 1856, where he served as a city councilman and on the Board of Education. As the Civil War loomed, he organized black volunteers for the Union army, assembling the Massachusetts 54th, the nation's first black regiment, and the Massachusetts 55th and the 5th Ohio. He also fought for the black vote, leading the National Equal Rights League in 1864 and carrying out far-reaching suffrage campaigns in Ohio, Kansas, and Missouri. In 1867, Congress approved suffrage for black males.

Traveling through the South as the educational inspector for the Freedmen's Bureau, Langston was an ardent spokesperson for educational opportunity, political equality, and economic justice for freedmen. In 1869, Langston organized the law department at Howard University in Washington, making it a hallmark of race and gender diversity. He served as acting president of Howard in 1872. In 1888 he became the first African-American elected to Congress from Virginia.

Zeta Phi Beta sorority

Founded on January 16, 1920, by Arizona Cleaver, Myrtle Tyler, Viola Tyler, Fannie Pettie, and Pearl Neal, Zeta departed from the traditional social model of sororities to form an organization predicated on the precepts of "Scholarship, Service, Sisterly Love and Finer Womanhood." The first international chapters were chartered in Monrovia, Liberia, in 1948.

Howard University: The Legacy Continues

Howard University's legacy of greatness spans more than a century, yet it brings generations closer as they share a common heritage and pride in a place that is more than the sum total of its buildings. Some would say this legacy results from the selfless sacrifice of the founders, who built the university, and those who followed in their footsteps; others attribute it to the visionary leadership of people such as Albert I. Cassell, who designed the campus as it is today. Still others will say Howard's legacy is its students and faculty, the thoughts and ideas exchanged in the buildings, the relationships built. . . . Or perhaps it is found in a motto, "Equal Rights and Education for All," embodying a concept so profound that it inspired a social revolution that continues to this very day.

For wherever and whenever measures are advanced for the welfare of the people

and the direction of the masses there the [children] of Howard will be found

in the midst of them . . .

—Professor Kelly Miller,
President's Address, Sixth Triennial Meeting of the College Alumni Association
of Howard University, College Chapel, May 18, 1892

INDEX